HEINEMANN HISTORY

THE FRENCH REVOLUTION

STUDY UNITS

D1386792

HEINEMANN EDUCATIONAL

Peter Mantin

Heinemann Educational Publishers
Halley Court, Jordan Hill, Oxford OX2 8EJ
Part of Harcourt Education
Heinemann is the registered trademark of
Harcourt Education Limited.

First published 1992

06

15 14 13

**British Library Cataloguing in Publication data for this title
is available from the British Library.**

ISBN 0 435 31282 0
ISBN 978 0 435 31282 4

Designed by Ron Kamen, Green Door Design Ltd.,
Basingstoke.

Illustrated by Phill Burrows, Jeff Edwards,

Printed in China

The front cover shows the storming of the Bastille
on 14 July, 1789.

Acknowledgements

The author and publisher would like to thank the following for
permission to reproduce photographs:

Bibliothèque Nationale, Paris: 4.4B
Bildarchiv Preussischer Kulturbesitz, Berlin: 4.3B
Bowes Museum: 2.6D
Bridgeman Art Library: p.32, 1.1A, 1.3H, 1.3I
Bridgemen Art Library/Giraudon: cover
By courtesy of the Trustees of the British Museum: 2.5B, 2.7G,
3.1C, 3.7A, 4.1B, 4.4A, 4.4C
Bulloz: 2.4A, 2.8A
J. Allan Cash: 3.6C
Jean-Loup Charmet, Paris: 1.2C and p.35, 2.4B, 2.7F, 2.8D,
3.3C, 3.6A
C. M. Dixon: 3.4B

E. T. Archive: 2.2D, 2.6C, 2.7A, 3.2B
Garden Picture Library/Nigel Temple: 1.3J
Giraudon: 1.3A, 1.3C, 2.1A and p.34, 2.8B, 2.8C, 3.4F
Hubert Josse, Paris: 2.2A and p.35, 3.1A, 3.2C, 3.5A, 4.5B
S. and M. Matthews: 3.3B
Musée du Louvre/Christian Larrieu: 3.4A
Reunion: 2.7D, 3.5C
Every effort has been made to contact copyright holders of the
material reproduced in this book. Any omissions will be
rectified in subsequent printings if notice is given to the
publisher.

Research help: Roger Butterworth

Details of written sources

In many sources the wording or sentence has been simplified
to ensure that the source is accessible.

C. Barnett, *Bonaparte*, Allen and Unwin, 1978: 3.3A, 4.3D,
4.4D, 4.4E
Edmund Burke, *Reflections on the Revolution in France*, 1790,
Penguin, 1982: 2.5A
R. Cobb and C. Jones (Eds.), *Voices of the French Revolution*,
Salem House Publishers, 1988: 2.6A, 2.6B
L. Cowie, *Eighteenth Century Europe*, G. Bell, 1989: 1.3D
L. Cowie, *The French Revolution*, MacMillan, 1987: 1.3F, 1.3G
Michael Glover, *Napoleonic Wars*, Book Club Associates,
1979: 3.2E, 4.2B
Michael Glover, *Warfare in the Age of Bonaparte*, Book Club
Associates, 1980: 3.2D
J. Hanoteau (H. Miles, Trans.), *Memoirs of General de
Caulaincourt*, Duke of Vicenza, 1812-13, Cassell, 1935: 3.1B,
3.1E, 4.3A, 4.3C
J. C. Herold, *The Age of Napoleon*, Penguin, 1969: 3.2A, 3.5B,
3.6D, 3.6E, 4.1A
C. Hibbert, *Days of the French Revolution*, Penguin, 1989: 2.7B
R. M. Johnston (Ed.), *The Corsican, a Diary of Napoleon's Life
in His Own Words*, Houghton Mifflin Co., 1910: 4.5A
C. A. Leeds, *European History, 1789-1914*, M and E
Handbooks, 1989: 2.5C, 3.7B
Paul de Remusat (Ed.) (H. Miles, Trans.), *Memoirs of Madame
de Remusat*, 1802-8, Sampson and Low, 1881: 3.1D
Emmanuel-Joseph Sieyes, *What is the Third Estate?*, 1789: 1.2
R. J. Unstead, *A History of the World*, A & C Black, 1983: 2.2B
B. Wright, *Revolution and Terror*, Longman, 1989: 2.2C

CONTENTS

1.1 Europe in 1780

There are many differences between Europe in 1780 and Europe today. Many important and powerful European countries were run by kings or emperors. In the Middle Ages these rulers had claimed that their power came from God. By 1780 monarchs no longer claimed to be appointed by God. However, many of them had come to believe in **absolute monarchies**, that is, countries run by monarchs who had complete power and did not share it with a parliament.

France was a powerful and important country. In 1763 France had to surrender most of its overseas empire to Britain after it had been beaten in the Seven Years' War. France was ruled by the Bourbon family. King Louis XVI (1754–93) was an absolute monarch. There was an important 'middle' class of businessmen, traders, lawyers and doctors, but most of them weren't allowed to be involved in government.

Prussia was ruled by Frederick the Great (1712–86). He was also an absolute monarch. He had spent many years of his reign fighting wars. In 1740 he had taken the important province of Silesia from Austria. After that time Prussia became more and more powerful in what is now northern Germany.

The Habsburg family ruled an **empire** which included the Austrian Netherlands, Austria and Hungary. It had been the most powerful in central Europe until Frederick the Great challenged its power. This empire was not united, for example more than twenty different languages were spoken in it. The Emperor Joseph II ruled these lands as an absolute monarch. But not everyone was happy with his rule. In 1787 there was a rebellion in the Austrian Netherlands by Belgians who did not like the way Joseph was ruling the Empire, and controlling it from far away in Vienna.

A SOURCE

King Louis XVI in his coronation robes. This was painted by Duplessis (1725–1802).

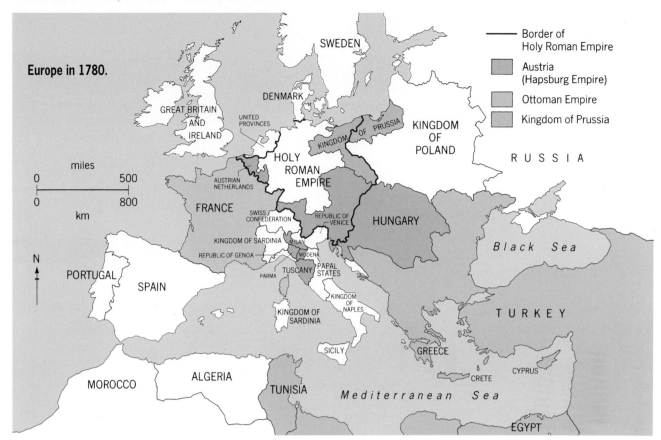

Europe in 1780.

Legend:
— Border of Holy Roman Empire
Austria (Hapsburg Empire)
Ottoman Empire
Kingdom of Prussia

Russia was a huge country which had become more involved in European affairs under Peter the Great (1682–1725). The Empress Catherine the Great (1729–96) was another absolute monarch. Russia had taken land from Poland, Turkey and Sweden. In Russia, farming methods were old-fashioned; there were often bad harvests and famine. The labourers who worked on the land were known as **serfs**. They were little more than slaves of their masters. Russia, too, had seen rebellion in 1773 when a Cossack called Pugachev led a rebellion of serfs. It was brutally crushed by the army in 1774.

Britain was very different from the continental countries. George III (1738–1820) was not an absolute monarch. He had to share power with parliament, which made and discussed the laws of the land. Britain was a rich and powerful country which had its industrial revolution before the continental countries did. It also had a strong navy and had built up a large overseas empire.

In 1776 Britain's American colonies declared themselves independent. Their revolt succeeded and Britain was forced to grant them independence in 1783. Britain did not have any major revolts at home. There were riots, however. In 1780, for example, over 400 people died in the religious disturbances known as the Gordon Riots.

Activities...

1 What does Source A suggest to you about how important Louis XVI considered himself to be?

2 Make a list, in chronological order, of the riots, rebellions or revolutions mentioned in this unit.

3 Compare the map of Europe in 1780 with a modern map of Europe.
   a Make a list of the countries that existed in 1780 but don't today.
   b Make a list of the countries that exist today but didn't in 1780.

1.2 The Three Estates

Today we believe in a system where everyone is treated equally by the law. But this was not the case in France before the Revolution. The French people belonged to one of three classes, or **estates**. Each estate had its own place in French society.

The **First Estate** was made up of members of the Church (the clergy). In 1789 the French Church was very important. It owned about one tenth of the land in France and some of its leaders, such as Cardinal Fleury, played a very important part in the government. Yet of the 130,000 clergy in France, most were parish priests who were quite poor. The Church was very important in an age when most people believed in heaven and hell. In return for praying for the King and the people, the First Estate was allowed **privileges**. Its members did not have to pay the *taille* (the main tax). They could not be called up for military service. If they broke the law they were tried in their own courts.

The **Second Estate** was made up of the nobles of France. In 1789 there were about 400,000 nobles in France. They owned about one third of the land. The older noble families had served the king for centuries – in battle, at court and in government jobs. Some noble families had fallen on hard times. They had been left behind by the newer noble families who had done well in business and bought their way into the nobility. Rich or poor, the nobility were expected to serve the King in war. In return they were granted privileges. For example, they did not have to pay many taxes to the government.

The **Third Estate** comprised most of the population, ranging from rich businessmen and professionals to poor peasants. The members of this estate had no privileges and played no part in running the country.

A **SOURCE**

The Third Estate forms nineteen-twentieths of the population. It does all the work that the privileged estates refuse to do. Well-paid and honourable positions are reserved for the privileged.

From 'What is the Third Estate?' by Emmanuel-Joseph Sieyès, 1789. He was a churchman who did not agree with the government.

B **SOURCE**

None are so wretched and downtrodden as the lower clergy. While the Bishop plays the great nobleman and spends huge sums on hounds, horses, furniture, servants, food and carriages, the parish priest cannot afford to buy a new cassock. The priest has to collect the tithe, but the Bishops, not he, pocket it. The Bishops treat their priests like stable boys.

From 'An enslaved France yearning for liberty' by Abbé Michel Lavassor.

Taxes
The *taille* was a tax on either land or income which neither the First nor Second Estates had to pay.

The *gabelle* was a special tax on salt. Today it seems an unusual tax, but in 1780 salt was an essential part of everyday life. It was used as a preservative for meat, and also to disguise the taste of stale food.

Tithes were taxes of one tenth of yearly income or produce paid to the Church.

Most of the people in the Third Estate were peasants, who made up 80% of the population of France. They had a hard life. Most of them did not own the land they farmed. As well as paying rent, they had to work free of charge for the local landowner on certain days of the year. They had to pay taxes to the government, like the *taille* and the *gabelle* (salt tax) and tithes to the Church. Sometimes they paid three quarters of their yearly income in taxes. They were also expected to fight whenever France went to war.

French cartoon, about 1789. The peasant is being crushed by a stone. 'Impots' were taxes and 'corvées' was forced labour.

Activities...

1 Look at Source C.
   a Which estate does the man under the stone represent? Explain your answer.
   b Which estates do the men on the stone represent? Explain your answer.

2 What point do you think the person who drew Source C was trying to make?

3 Using the information in this unit draw a diagram to show the place in society of the three estates.

4 What clues can you find in this unit to help explain why there was a revolution in France?

C

SOURCE

1.3 The Monarchy

French kings were **absolute monarchs**. Their powers were not limited by other people or groups, so they felt that they did not have to answer to the people for what they did. But they did think that they had to answer to God and that they had duties and obligations. One of these was to ensure respect for God. Another of the King's duties was to defend his people and make sure that people respected the law. The people also expected kings to rule by the law of the land. Monarchs who didn't do this were called **despots**.

For some French people a good example of a great king was **Louis XIV**. He came to the throne in 1643 when he was only four years old. In his early years he relied on his chief minister, **Mazarin**. From 1661, after Mazarin's death, Louis became more involved in the day-to-day government of the country, and made every part of the government answerable to him personally.

Louis XIV and his family, 1670 by Jean Nocret. The royal family are shown as gods and goddesses. Louis is seen second from the left as Apollo, the god of light.

B SOURCE

The King's bedroom is placed right at the centre of the palace. His rising and setting – the French *lever* and *coucher* apply to both monarchs and planets – were conducted in a blaze of public attention. The greatest nobles took it in turn to witness the event, pass the royal shirt, remove the royal stockings. The daily movements of the King seemed to match the movements of God's universe.

This was essential, for the King was not just the King, he was the state. The palace was built to stun the visitor into admiration.

From 'Architecture of the Western World', edited by M. Raeburn, 1980.

C SOURCE

Louis XIV's bedchamber, Versailles. The palace was redesigned by Jules Mansart and decorated by Charles Le Brun in the 1680s.

Louis XIV was an intelligent man. He was prepared to work very hard and was not afraid to make difficult decisions. His armies won many battles. Under his leadership France was feared and respected as the greatest power in Europe.

The Palace of Versailles, outside Paris, still stands as a monument to Louis XIV. Versailles had been a fairly small hunting lodge. In 1661 Louis XIV employed the architect Louis LeVau to build a palace fit for the King and his court.

The front of the building is 402 metres long. The central section alone is 73 metres long. Magnificent furniture, decorations and art treasures made Versailles the wonder of the age. The finest musicians, artists and writers came to the court of the 'Sun King', as Louis XIV was known. French nobles were encouraged to come to court to pay their respects to the King. This meant the King could keep an eye on powerful nobles who might challenge his rule.

Louis XIV died in 1715, having reigned for 72 years. He had dazzled the people of Europe, but left France in financial ruin with his extravagance at court and his costly wars. His son, Louis XV, was a weaker king who allowed the country's finances to slide further into chaos (see Source D).

D SOURCE

The King's [Louis XV's] ministers have a strong influence on his decisions, for he refers almost everything to them. The ministers can do almost as they wish.

From the Duc de Croy's diary, 1747.

Activities...

1 Study Source C.
   a What is it?
   b Who made it?
   c Describe what it shows.
   d Who ordered it to be made?
   e When was it made?
   f Why might it have been made?

2 Versailles cost vast sums of money to build. Why do you think Louis XIV built such an enormous and costly palace?

3 Look at Source D. In what ways did Louis XV fail to live up to the standards set by Louis XIV?

Louis XVI came to the throne in 1774. Four years earlier he had married Marie Antoinette, the daughter of Maria Theresa, the Empress of Austria. The marriage was arranged by diplomats who wanted to strengthen the links between the two powerful royal families. At the time of the wedding, Louis was only 15 years old.

Louis XVI grew into a big man with a huge appetite. He would get up at six o'clock, eat four chops, a fat chicken, six eggs poached in meat juice, a slice of ham and drink a bottle and a half of champagne. Then he would get dressed, go out hunting and return hungry again.

In 1778 the Queen gave birth to a daughter. A son was born in 1781 and another in 1785. Louis was a proud father and enjoyed spending time with his children. It was a terrible blow to him when his eldest son died from tuberculosis at the age of eight. The royal couple were so upset that they stopped their public appearances. Only a few courtiers were allowed to see the unhappy King. Unluckily for Louis this tragedy took place less than a month before the dramatic, revolutionary events of July 1789.

E

He did not have the qualities needed by a man born to be a leader. He was timid and lacked self confidence. It was soon recognized that others could influence his decisions.

Statement about Louis XVI by a noble member of the parlement (law court) of Paris.

Activities...

4 a Make a list of Louis XVI's good points
b How useful would these good points be for the job of running France as an absolute monarch?
c Make a list of Louis XVI's bad points.
d How much of a problem would these bad points be for the job of running France as an absolute monarch? Explain your answer.

5 In what ways did Louis XVI fail to live up to the example set by Louis XIV (Source E)?

F

Louis XVI is seen passing his mornings in his closet observing with his telescope those who arrive at Versailles. He often occupies himself in sweeping, nailing and unnailing. Some common sense, simple tastes an honest heart: that is his good side. He tends not to be able to make his mind up and he is weak willed: there is the contrast.

From the journal of the Abbé de Veri, 1775.

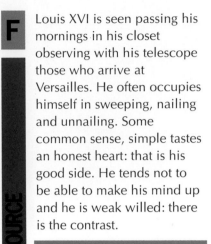

G

The public at first viewed with pleasure the King's gift of the Trianon to the Queen; but it began to be disturbed and alarmed by the money spent by Her Majesty there. By her order the gardens have been completely changed into the style of an English garden, which cost at least 150,000 livres. The Queen has had a theatre built at the Trianon; she has only presented one play there, followed by supper, but this entertainment was very expensive.

The Queen's allowance has been doubled, and yet she has debts. She has bought many diamonds, and her card playing has become very costly.

Letter from the Austrian ambassador at Versailles, to Marie Antoinette's mother, 1776. At this time a French peasant probably earned around 600 livres a year.

H

SOURCE

Louis XVI gave Marie Antoinette her own palace called the Petit Trianon. She spent huge sums of money creating her own village which was surrounded by beautiful gardens. This late 18th-century painting shows the village.

I

SOURCE

Part of the garden at the Petit Trianon illuminated at night, from a contemporary painting.

J

SOURCE

A modern photo of one of the buildings in the gardens of the Petit Trianon.

Activities...

6 a Look carefully at Sources H, I and J. Which two pictures show the same place at the Petit Trianon? What is the place?

b 'It was like an 18th-century Disneyland.' Do you agree with this description of the Petit Trianon?

c Taxes in France were high. The monarchy was short of money. What effect do you think that spending on the Petit Trianon had on French people's views of the monarchy?

1.4 The King in Debt and Danger

Louis XVI was facing financial ruin in the early 1780s. One problem seemed to lead to another and it was difficult to find a way out. You can see from the diagram that the French government was spending more than it could afford. Louis needed **money** to pay for his court, his government officials, his solicitors and his debts. If he couldn't find the money there was a real danger that government might break down, or that the King might have to depend too much on the nobles or on people he owed money to.

The King could raise money by **taxation**, but we have already seen that the first two Estates didn't pay many taxes and the Third Estate had to pay more than most of its members could afford (see pages 6–7).

Another way in which the King raised money was by selling **offices**. These were government jobs which allowed the holder of the job to have a title, which could be passed on from father to son. In 18th-century France, between 30,000 and 50,000 people are thought to have entered the nobility in this way.

In the past the King and his government had got hold of money by **borrowing** it from wealthy people. When the government paid back the loan, it had to pay **interest** on it. This meant the government paid back more money than it originally borrowed. **Lenders** made money by charging high interest.

Over the years the King had borrowed huge amounts of money. In 1788 50% of all the government's spending went just on paying interest to people who had loaned it money. This cost twice as much money as running the French army and navy. Things were getting out of control.

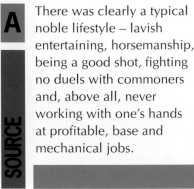

A SOURCE

There was clearly a typical noble lifestyle – lavish entertaining, horsemanship, being a good shot, fighting no duels with commoners and, above all, never working with one's hands at profitable, base and mechanical jobs.

From 'L'Ancien Régime' by Pierre Goubert, 1969.

B SOURCE

The population of France was increasing ... The 1770s and 1780s were years of by poor harvests ... As the amount of grain available to feed the enlarged population went down, so its price rose; and there was no comparable rise in wages. The cost of food took up a large amount of the total wage, leaving little to buy other goods. That led to problems for industry and many people became unemployed. In such an economic climate it was more difficult than ever for the government to raise the money it needed.

From 'France before the Revolution' by J. H. Shennan, 1983.

The King could not afford to let this debt get any bigger. He was having trouble paying it as it was. As well as this it was becoming difficult to find enough people who were willing to lend money to the government. By 1789 the King knew that he had to find a way of getting more money without borrowing it. If he could not find a way then the French government would collapse.

Government income and spending, 1786.

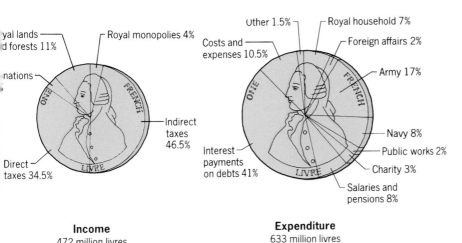

Royal lands and forests 11%
Royal monopolies 4%
nations
FRENCH
Indirect taxes 46.5%
Direct taxes 34.5%
LIVRE

Income
472 million livres

Other 1.5%
Costs and expenses 10.5%
Royal household 7%
Foreign affairs 2%
Army 17%
ONE
FRENCH
Navy 8%
Public works 2%
Interest payments on debts 41%
Charity 3%
LIVRE
Salaries and pensions 8%

Expenditure
633 million livres

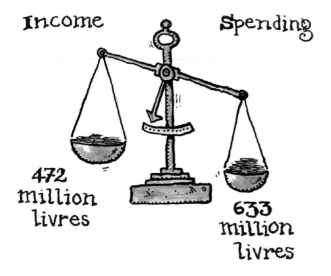

Income   Spending

472 million livres

633 million livres

Activities...

1 A vicious circle occurs when one problem leads to another as things go from bad to worse. Look at the diagram about government income and spending in 1786, then sketch out the vicious circle of economic problems facing the King.

2 a What were the advantages to the King of selling offices (jobs which allowed the holders to become titled nobles)?
 b What were the disadvantages of selling offices?

3 The diagram shows how bad the economic crisis was.
 a Write down the advantages and disadvantages of the following ways of solving the crisis:
  i borrow even more money
  ii make nobles and clergy pay taxes.
 b Could you have suggested to Louis XVI an alternative way of solving his crisis? Explain your answer.

4 Why might the problems described in Source B have made it more difficult for the King to raise money?

2.1 The Estates General

By 1787 the French government had been in debt for over one hundred years and the King needed to find a new way of raising money. The person responsible to the King for raising money was **Calonne**. He decided that the only way to raise more money was to tax the people in the First and Second Estates.

Calonne's idea was that people should pay tax depending on how much **land** they owned. People who owned more land would pay more tax. Obviously this was not popular with the people in the First and Second Estates. They were not used to paying taxes and did not want to start.

Calonne called a meeting of members of the First and Second Estates. This meeting was called the **Assembly of Notables**. He hoped that they would see how badly the King needed the money and agree to the land tax. Instead they said that such a tax could only be agreed by people from all the Estates meeting together. This was called the **Estates General** and it had not had a meeting since 1614.

The King was angry. He told the Assembly of Notables to stop meeting. He replaced Calonne with a man named **Brienne**. Brienne knew that if the new tax was ever going to work he had to get the agreement of the *Parlement* of Paris. This was the Paris law court. It was controlled by nobles.

Like Calonne, Brienne was soon in trouble. The *Parlement* of Paris refused to agree to the new tax. They too said that only the Estates General could agree to such an idea. The angry King dismissed the members of the *Parlement*.

Things were getting desperate. The King needed money badly. In the country, people were unhappy. In 1788 the harvest had been very bad. The price of a loaf of bread went up by 50% between April 1788 and March 1789. There were riots and the country was becoming impossible to run. At last the King gave way. He called a meeting of the Estates General. The King hoped that this meeting would help him raise money.

However some of the people who came to the Estates General had plans of their own. These were **middle-class** people from the Third Estate such as magistrates, lawyers, teachers and bankers. They wanted a say in how France was governed.

Food crisis
Throughout the winter of 1788 there were violent riots in different parts of the country. Summer hailstorms had been followed by drought. The winter had brought freezing weather, followed by flooding. The bad harvest had caused the price of bread to soar, and some landowners were profiteering, by keeping their corn until prices rose further.

***Parlement* of Paris**
This was the Supreme Court of France. It had originally been a group of nobles and church people who gave advice to the king. By the 18th century many nobles paid to be a member. It had power over much of France. It 'Registered' the orders given by the King. This meant it said whether these ideas should become law. Often the *Parlement* tried to stop any ideas which would reduce the power and wealth of the rich.

Assembly of Notables
This was a group of people from the First and Second Estates. They were rich and usually supported what the King wanted.

Contemporary painting of the Tennis Court Oath by Jacques-Louis David. David was an enthusiastic supporter of the Revolution.

Estates General

This was a group which represented all the different estates in France. The King called this meeting when he wanted people to agree to new taxes. In 1789 the King's new finance minister, **Necker**, advised him to double the number of people from the Third Estate. As they stood for the majority of people in France, they would want to tax the nobles.

The Estates General met in May 1789. The middle-class people demanded a share of power. They demanded a **constitution**. This was a set of rules which said how the country should be run. Even the King would have to obey these rules. Many of these ideas were opposed by the King and by the richest members of the First and Second Estates. When the King tried to break up the meeting, members of the Third Estate met in a nearby tennis court. They pledged not to go home until France had a constitution. They called themselves the **National Assembly**. This was on 20 June, 1789. Historians call this pledge **The Tennis Court Oath**.

Activities...

1 a The Assembly of Notables and the Third Estate both opposed the King. Explain the different reasons they had for doing this.

 b Explain how these different reasons caused trouble for the King.

2 'The King's bad government was to blame for the unrest in France in 1789.'
Using the evidence in this unit say whether you think this is a fair comment.

3 In what ways could Source A be useful to a historian?

A

Painting of the storming of the Bastille, made soon after the event, by Cholat, a man who had taken part in it.

The middle-class members of the National Assembly did not at first plan to make a **democracy** – a sharing of power with all the people in the country. They wanted some of the power for themselves.

On 27 June, King Louis ordered members of the First and Second Estates to join the National Assembly. Some people thought that the revolt against the King would soon be over. They had got what they wanted.

Things soon went much further than these people had intended. Many **working-class people** and **peasants** wanted much greater changes in how France was run. Because of the bad harvest in 1788 food prices continued to rise. Ordinary people wanted more action to improve their lives. As the National Assembly talked they began to take action themselves. They were encouraged by what the middle class had got away with.

B

SOURCE

The fall of the Bastille was important for two reasons: it had long been a symbol of royal power and its soldiers offered no resistance to the mob.

From 'A History of the World' by R. J. Unstead, 1983.

C

SOURCE

The events of July [in Paris] marked the end of absolute royal power. Revolutions took place in other towns. The middle-class leaders in Paris usually showed respect for private property. But the peasants attacked property.

From 'Revolution and Terror in France' by B. Wright, 1989.

A contemporary engraving showing the fall of the Bastille.

In Paris there were fears that the King was going to get rid of the National Assembly. Everyone knew he had wanted to do so before but was afraid of stirring up more trouble. The National Assembly was unable to control the working people of Paris. A crowd of 8000 of them broke into a building called the **Invalides**. They captured weapons and on July 14 they marched to the fortress of the Bastille.

This fortress was used by the King as a prison. To many people the Bastille stood for all that was wrong in the way France was run. It was a **symbol** of the King and his government. They wanted to destroy it.

The governor of the Bastille, the **Marquis de Launay**, refused to hand the fortress over to the people and the crowd attacked the prison. Although there were many soldiers in and around Paris they refused to stop this attack. Louis was losing control of the army, too.

The crowd captured the Bastille and cut off the governor's head. They found that there were only seven prisoners inside. Despite this many people were excited by this victory. In July and August, workers and peasants all over France attacked the powerful and rich. The revolution was both spreading and getting more violent.

Activities...

1 How useful is Source A for discovering what happened at the fall of the Bastille?

2 The National Assembly had defied the King. The people of Paris who stormed the Bastille were defying the King. Does this mean that members of the National Assembly must have approved of the storming of the Bastille? Give reasons for your answer.

3 Many people in France still celebrate the fall of the Bastille as a great event in the revolution. But there were only seven prisoners held there! Does this mean that people today are wrong to think it was important? Explain your answer.

2.3 1789 – The Year of Revolution

The fall of the Bastille sparked off violence all across France. There were many uprisings by peasants. The summer of 1789 was called the **Grand Peur** (Great Fear). Peasants attacked the houses of rich landowners, broke down fences and killed their animals. They burnt the records which said how much rent and tax the peasants had to pay.

These violent acts were encouraged by a group of people who called themselves the **Jacobins**. They said that peasants should no longer do what the landowners told them to do.

The attempt by the better-off members of the Third Estate to share power with the nobles had started off a series of events which they had never planned. It had encouraged the poorer people to rise up in revolt. A revolution (when a new class gets into power) was beginning to take place. The National Assembly was no longer in control. The middle-class members became very worried about what was happening.

The Church people of the First Estate and the nobles of the Second Estate realized that power was beginning to slip from their hands, too. They realized that their control over the peasants in the countryside was being lost. However it was hard to stop this happening once it had started.

King Louis XVI was very angry. He even thought about sending soldiers to recapture the Bastille. His advisers told him this was a bad idea. They said that he could no longer rely on his soldiers to do as he ordered. Louis allowed the people of Paris to do as they wanted. A new government of the city (the *Paris Commune*) was set up by some members of the Third Estate.

On 4 August 1789 the National Assembly tried to do away with the things that were making the peasants so angry. A new law ended many of the powers of the nobles and the Church. This stopped them punishing peasants in their own private courts, and taking taxes and **tithes** from them. All adult citizens were given the right to vote. On 26 August they produced a **Declaration of the Rights of Man**. This promised freedom to the people of France. This still did not stop the violence. In October a crowd marched from Paris to the Palace of Versailles and forced the King and his family to return to Paris.

Activities...

1 a Look at the information in this unit and in Units 2.1 and 2.2. Make a timeline of the months from January to December 1789. On your timeline mark the main events mentioned in these three units.

b The cartoon shows **causes** (events which make other things happen) and **effects** (events which are the result of other things happening). Which of the changes shown in the cartoon do you think are **causes** and which **effects**? How did you make your decision?

2 a Explain what the following people might have felt about the laws passed in August 1789 :
- the King
- a poor peasant
- a rich noble
- a church leader.

b Does the evidence in this unit suggest that the members of the Third Estate planned a revolution?

3 What are the strengths and weaknesses of using a cartoon like the one in this unit as evidence about what happened in the past?

2.4 A New France

Between 1789 and 1793 there were many changes in the way that France was governed. During these years the powers and privileges of the King, the nobles and the Church were removed. This was popular with many people who in the past had had to pay heavy taxes and do most of the work

These changes were carried out by the **legislature**. At first this was the **National Assembly**, then, after September 1792, the **Convention** and in 1793 the **Committee of Public Safety**. These were all different experiments in ways to govern and change France. It was not easy to carry out these changes. In 1789 law and order had broken down in many parts of France. Some people were in favour of the King, nobles and Church – others were against them. After April 1792 France was at war. People's ideas became more extreme and more violent. The changes which had begun with old laws and ways of running the country now became a matter of life or death.

Perhaps the most important change was that people had political power who had never had any before. This went far beyond the aims of many of those who swore the Tennis Court Oath in 1789. They had started something which went much further than many of them could ever have imagined.

During 1790 and 1791 the National Assembly brought in many new laws, abolishing many of the most unpopular taxes and changing voting rights.

Changes brought about by the National Assembly, 1789–91

- Special **privileges of the nobles** were abolished. Inherited titles such as prince, baron, duc were no longer recognized. Coats of arms were banned.
- The King had to accept a **'Civil Constitution of the Clergy'**. Churchmen were to be elected public officials and had to answer to the government for what they did.
- **Church lands were taken over** and became public property.
- **New paper money** called *assignats* was introduced, but this soon lost its value in the inflation which followed the Revolution. Poor people didn't benefit from the new money any more than they had done from the old.
- Some of the old **Church land was sold** at low prices to the peasants, but most of the land was bought up by merchants, bankers and other people who were rich before the Revolution.
- **Judges had to be elected**. Before the Revolution, judges could buy their jobs.

A

SOURCE

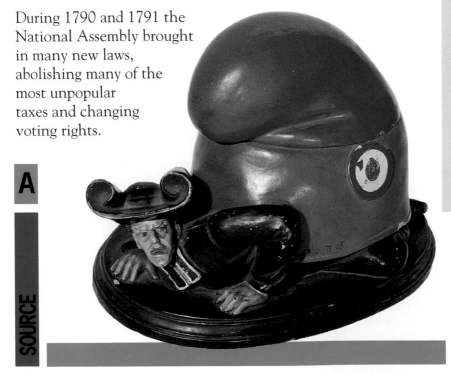

Inkwell showing a priest being crushed by the red cap of liberty. The idea for the cap came from ancient Rome, where freed slaves wore a special cap.

A new **constitution** was introduced. A constitution is a set of laws or ideas for the running of a country. The new constitution meant that the King would have to accept restrictions on his power. He would no longer be an absolute monarch. The legislature would make the laws. From now on the King would have to accept laws he didn't like. Tax-paying citizens would be given the right to vote for members of the legislature. Most poor people would still not have the right to vote, even though they paid taxes.

Activities...

1 Look at Source B.
   a Which sorts of people were likely to benefit from these freedoms. How?
   b Who would not benefit from these changes?

2 Make a list of the changes described in this unit.

3 Did the Revolution change everything or did some things stay the same? Explain your answer.

4 Which do you think was the most important change? Why?

5 What do you think the people who brought in these changes were trying to do?

B **SOURCE**

Playing cards showing some of the new freedoms in France:
* *freedom of the press*
* *freedom of marriage*
* *equality of work*
* *equality of colour*
* *freedom of religion.*

2.5 From Revolution to War

In June 1791 the King and the royal family tried to escape from the Tuileries Palace in Paris and leave France. They sought help from French princes across the French border and from the Emperor of Austria. They only got as far as the village of Varennes before they were recognized and brought back. Many French people lost confidence in the King.

Despite these events the other kings and queens of Europe did not seem too worried by the Revolution – especially as the new Assembly declared that war was not one of its aims. However, they soon began to change their minds.

In March 1791 Francis II became the Emperor of Austria. More militant than his father, he was keen to fight against the French people in defence of their King and Queen. In August 1791 the rulers of Austria and Prussia met. Although they had been enemies for years, they agreed to join forces to help the French King if Britain would back them.

When the Revolution had broken out a number of French noblemen emigrated (left the country). They were known as *emigrés*. Some of them formed an army on France's eastern border. Their leader was the King's brother, the Comte d'Artois. When the revolutionary National Assembly voted in 1790 to end the titles of the nobles, this made some of the **emigrés** even more determined to fight.

In April 1792 France declared war on Austria. Food was short in France. There was unemployment and crime. In July the Austrian Duke of Brunswick threatened to destroy Paris if the royal family were hurt. He invaded France in August. French troops were beaten in two clashes with the Austrians. Rumours of an Austrian attack on Paris spread quickly. In this atmosphere of fear and panic, around 1000 prisoners suspected of supporting the Austrians were killed. These **September Massacres** disgusted people in many parts of Europe. Cartoons like the one in Source B began to appear in Britain.

In November 1792 the French government issued the **Edict of Fraternity**. This offered help to other peoples of Europe who tried to have their own revolutions. French generals were ordered to end feudal rights in lands they conquered, and to take away the property of nobles and churchmen.

Some ideas of the French Revolutionaries

1 **Liberty, equality, fraternity.** The Declaration of the Rights of Man, August 1789, stated that all people were born free and equal.
2 **Sovereignty.** The people should be allowed to rule themselves.
3 **Free speech**, freedom of **religion**, **freedom of the press** were held to be human rights for all people.

SOURCE A

Is our monarchy to be destroyed, with all the laws and old customs of the kingdom? Is the House of Lords to be voted useless? Are the bishops to be got rid of? Are the Church lands to be sold to Jews? Are all ranks and titles to be ended. Will law and order break down? Will the country go bankrupt?

From 'Reflections on the Revolution in France' by Edmund Burke, 1790. Burke is wondering what would happen if Britain were to have a revolution. The book sold many copies in Britain and was also read by many French emigrés.

Petion

Vive la Liberté   Vive la Égalité

Sans le Grand

Propriété de la Nation

Un petit Souper, a la Parisienne:____or____A Family of Sans Culotts refreshing, after the fatigues of the day.

James Gillray's 1792 cartoon warning of the dangers of the French Revolution.

France was in the midst of famine and lawlessness. Unemployment was high as industry had collapsed. Marat observed that war was needed to 'rid France of 300,000 armed criminals'.

From 'European History, 1789–1914' by C. A. Leeds, 1989. Marat was one of the French revolutionary leaders.

Activities...

1 What were:
  a the flight to Varennes?
  b the September Massacres?

2 Make a list of the things in Source A that worried Burke.

3 Explain how each of the following factors may have helped to cause war between France and other European countries by 1793:
  a the ideas of Edmund Burke.
  b Francis II became the Emperor of Austria.
  c economic problems in France.
  d French *emigrés*.
  e the Edict of Fraternity.

  f instructions to French generals.
  g revolutionary ideas.

4 Were these factors of equal importance or were some more important than others? Explain your answer.

5 What point was the person who drew Source B trying to make? Support your answer with examples from the cartoon.

6 Did the French Revolution make war with other European countries inevitable? Give reasons for your answer.

2.6 The Execution of the King

Under the Constitution of 1791 Louis XVI became simply 'king of the French' (instead of 'King of France'). He was no longer an absolute monarch. He did not feel comfortable in this new France and with this new position.

- On 20 June 1791 he attempted to escape from Paris and leave France, but was captured at Varennes (see Unit 2.5).
- This led to calls for France to become a republic (a country without a king).
- In the spring of 1792 the Austrian Duke of Brunswick invaded France and threatened to destroy Paris if members of the royal family were harmed.
- Louis was accused of being a traitor who did not do enough to protect his country against foreign invasion.
- On 10 August an angry crowd attacked the King's Tuileries Palace. About 1200 people were killed.
- Louis and his family were imprisoned. On 21 September a new Convention (parliament) was set up. It voted for a republic.
- In December 1792 Louis XVI was put on trial. He was accused of plotting against the French nation and helping the Austrian invasion. He was found guilty and sentenced to death.

On 21 January 1793 'Louis Capet', the former King Louis XVI of France, was executed at the *Place de la Revolution* in Paris. The sources in this unit describe different points of view about the events of that day.

A His blood flows; cries of joy from 80,000 armed men rend the air. His blood flows and there are people who dip a fingertip, a quill, a scrap of paper in it. One tastes it: 'It is vilely salt!' An executioner at the scaffold side sells small bundles of his hair; people buy the ribbon that tied it. Everyone carries off a small bundle of his clothing or some other blood-stained remnant. The whole populace go by, arm in arm, laughing and talking as if from some festivity. The taverns on the bloody square had their wine bottles emptied as usual. They sold cakes and patties around the beheaded body, which was put in the wicker basket of the common criminal.

SOURCE

Description of the execution of Louis XVI, by Mercier, a Deputy to the Convention. The Convention had voted by a clear majority for the execution of the King. Mercier was in the crowd which witnessed the execution.

B Louis XVI lost his life on Monday, at half past ten in the morning, and to the very last he maintained the greatest possible courage.

He wished to speak to the people from the scaffold, but was seized by the executioners, who were following their orders, and who pushed him straight under the fatal blade. He was able to speak only these words, in a very strong voice: 'I forgive my enemies; I trust that my death will be for the happiness of my people, but I grieve for France and I fear that she may suffer the anger of the Lord.'

The King took off his coat himself at the foot of the scaffold, and when someone sought to help him he said cheerfully, 'I do not need any help.' He also refused help to climb onto the scaffold, and went up with a firm, brisk step.

After his death his body and head were immediately taken to the parish cemetery and thrown into a pit fifteen feet deep, where they were consumed by quicklime. And so there remains nothing of this unhappy prince except the memory of his virtues and his misfortune.

SOURCE

From a letter from Bernard, a supporter of the King, to his mother, 23 January 1793.

Engraving of the execution of Louis XVI. It is not known who painted it or when it was painted.

Plate showing the execution of Louis XVI. It was made soon after the execution. Plates like these were often sold as souvenirs.

Activities...

1 Which points from Source B does the author of Source A seem to ignore?

2 If you only had Source A to go on, what would you think about the execution of Louis XVI?

3 Which do you find more convincing, Source A or Source B? Explain why you made this choice.

4 What questions would you want to ask about the person who made Source C, to find out if you could trust it as evidence about the execution of Louis XVI? Explain your answer.

5 Source D is just a plate. Does that mean an historian studying Louis XVI's execution will not find it as useful as the engraving (Source C)? Give reasons.

2.7 The Terror

The period of French history between 1793 and 1795 has been called the **Reign of Terror**. What was it like to live in France during that time?

Early in 1793 France was fighting a war against six European countries – Austria, Prussia, Spain, Sardinia, Britain and Holland. These countries had joined together into a **coalition** to fight France because they wanted to destroy the new French Republic. In March 1793 the French army was beaten by the Austrians at the battle of Neerwinden. The French commander Dumouriez was one of two commanders who went over to the Austrian side. He said that the revolutionary government was being run by 'idiots and scoundrels'.

These military threats helped cause new rumours of a royalist plot to overthrow the Revolution. Rebels in Toulon declared that the Dauphin (son of Louis XVI) was the true king. British forces supported the rebels. In the Vendée (a region of Western France) there was a serious and bloody rising against the Revolution.

The price of bread began to rise again. This offered a threat to the Revolution. The new paper currency, the *assignat*, lost almost 80% of its original value. There were rumours that some people were hiding food and selling it later at a profit, whilst others went hungry.

A

SOURCE

Painting of prisoners brought before a revolutionary tribunal, 1794.

B

SOURCE

Jean Baptiste Henry, aged 18, journeyman tailor, convicted of having sawn down a tree of liberty, executed 6 September 1793.

Jean Julien, wagoner having been sentenced to twelve years hard labour, took it into his head to cry 'long live the King', brought back to the Tribunal and condemned to death.

Henriette Françoise Marboeuf, aged 55, convicted of having hoped for the arrival of the Austrians and Prussians and of keeping food for them, condemned to death and executed the same day.

François Bertrand, aged 37, publican, convicted of having provided the defenders of the country with sour wine, condemned to death and executed the same day.

Marie Plaisant, seamstress, convicted of having exclaimed that she was an aristocrat and that she did not care a fig for the nation, condemned to death and executed the same day.

From the 'Liste générale des Condamnés' (Execution Record), 1793.

The threat to the revolutionary government in 1793.

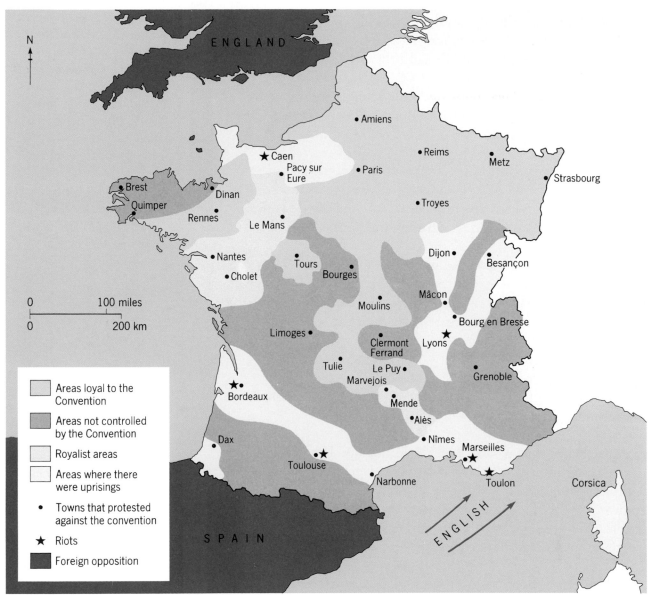

The **National Convention** (the parliament which had been set up in 1791) tried to deal with this crisis. In April 1793 it gave great powers to a **Committee of Public Safety**. The political group which controlled the Committee was the **Jacobins**. The leading figure in this Committee was Maximilien **Robespierre**. In June 1793 the Convention passed the **Law of Prairial**. By this law, juries were allowed to convict people without hearing any evidence. Revolutionary tribunals, like the one shown in Source A, had the power to award the death penalty for many different political crimes. Then in September 1793 the Convention passed the **Law of Suspects**. People could now be put in prison without trial.

Activities...

1 What were the causes of the Reign of Terror?

2 How did revolutionary justice work? Using Sources A and B describe what happened at a revolutionary tribunal.

The Terror continued during the autumn and winter of 1793. About 3000 executions took place in Paris, and about 14,000 in the rest of the country. One of the first to die was Queen Marie Antoinette, executed in October 1793 for treason. In Lyons, a Jacobin called Joseph Fouché thought that the guillotine was 'too slow', so he ordered that over 300 people be killed by cannon fire. A fellow Jacobin saw these killings and wrote sarcastically to a friend in Paris, 'What a delicious moment. How you would have enjoyed it! Worthy indeed of Liberty!'

At Nantes, barges containing 2000 people were towed out into the middle of the river Loire and scuttled. Everyone was drowned. Birds hovered above the water, eating the dead flesh. Fish were so contaminated that fishing was banned.

In Paris, thousands of people watched the executions. Women called *tricoteuses* did their knitting by the guillotine. People placed bets on the order in which the soldiers would bring the prisoners out of the *tumbrils* (carts) and onto the scaffold.

The Committee of Public Safety said that the Terror was needed to get rid of the royalists. One of the revolutionary leaders, Saint-Just, said, 'You must punish not just traitors, but the indifferent (people who don't care) as well.'

Eventually people got sick of all the killing and lost confidence in the Committee of Public Safety. Some were bold enough to complain about the horrible smell near the scaffold. There was an atmosphere of fear. Eight out of every ten people who died in the Terror were poor people and not rich nobles. Many were worried that they would be the next to die.

As the military situation improved and the Austrian threat became weaker there was not the same need for an 'emergency' government. Robespierre was blamed for the killings even though he had had the backing of the entire Convention. He was arrested, but the jailer refused to lock him up. Late that night he was arrested again at the *Hotel de Ville* (Paris Town Hall). In the scuffle he was shot in the face.

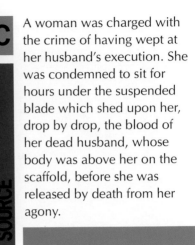

C A woman was charged with the crime of having wept at her husband's execution. She was condemned to sit for hours under the suspended blade which shed upon her, drop by drop, the blood of her dead husband, whose body was above her on the scaffold, before she was released by death from her agony.

SOURCE

Description of the Terror at Bordeaux.

D

SOURCE

Marie Antoinette, sketched by the painter David, on the way to her execution, 16 October 1793.

Next day Robespierre was taken to the scaffold. A woman shouted, 'You monster spewed out of hell. Go down to your grave with the curses of the wives and mothers of France. The thought of your execution makes me drunk with joy.'

Robespierre, the 'Incorruptible', fervent supporter of the Revolution, was executed in July 1794, the same death as all those others whose crime had been lack of commitment. From this point the worst of the Terror was over.

Hundreds of innocent people suffered, some through clerical mistakes. Others were sentenced after accusations by jealous or spiteful neighbours. One victim was fetched from prison to face a charge which had been brought against another prisoner with a similar name. Her protests were silenced by the prosecutor who said casually, 'Since she's here, we might just as well take her.' Another had lost his temper playing cards. When told off for not behaving like a good patriot, he shouted 'To hell with good patriots'. He was brought before the Tribunal, condemned and executed.

From 'The Days of the Revolution' by C. Hibbert, 1989.

The attempted assassination of Robespierre the night before his execution. From a 19th-century French painting.

The Zenith of French Glory; – The Pinnacle of Liberty.

'The Pinnacle of Liberty', by the British cartoonist, Gillray, published three weeks after the execution of Louis XVI.

Activities...

3 a List all the reasons for punishment in Sources B, C and E.
  b Put the list in order of seriousness.

4 Look at Source G.
  a Who do the people hanging from the lanterns represent?
  b Who does the man sitting on the lantern represent?
  c What point do you think the person who drew the cartoon was trying to make about the French Revolution? Explain your answer.

5 What do we learn from this unit about:
  a the people in charge of the revolutionary justice?
  b the people who died in the Terror?

2.8 Reaction

After the fall of Robespierre in July 1794, the policies of the government changed. The Terror was over, the power of the Jacobins was broken and a more moderate group took power. What was it like to live in Paris at that time?

Restaurants reopened. Those people who had money could sample the large number of new dishes made by the chefs, some of whom had learned their skills before the Revolution in the kitchens of noblemen. Large numbers of people were very poor. Some of them depended for food on what the restaurants threw away. Before and during the Revolution there had been both very poor and very rich people in Paris. Some of the 'new poor' were noblemen who had lost everything in the Revolution. Others were victims of inflation. They had been given the new *assignats*. As the economic crisis grew worse the paper money became less and less valuable.

Gambling clubs and the theatre prospered. There was also a craze, among both rich and poor people, for dancing. There were hundreds of dance halls – in old churches, gardens and palaces. The Church of St Sulpice was painted yellow. A dance floor was laid over the gravestones.

There were '*bals des victimes*'. These were dances given by relatives of people who had been guillotined during the Terror. The guests wore thin bands of blood-red silk around their necks, and cropped their hair at the back as if preparing for the guillotine.

During the Revolution, fashions had reflected the need for practicality and the desire for equality (see Source A). People gave up powdering their hair about 1790. At the end of the Terror there was a brief period of wildly extremist fashions among young people (see Source D). But the main fashion influence of the 1790s – in architecture as well as clothes – was the styles of the ancient Greeks and Romans (Source C). The red 'Liberty Bonnet' (worn by the sans culottes in Source A), which became a symbol of the Revolution, was modelled on the hats worn by freed Roman slaves.

*The **sans culottes**. 'Sans culottes' means 'without knee breeches'.*

A

The 'sans culottes' showed their support for the Revolution by rejecting the knee breeches and silk stockings of the nobles. Instead they wore plain trousers, short jackets, a scarf around the neck and a liberty cap. The women dressed with similar simplicity.

SOURCE

B An example of women's fashion before the Revolution.

D An '*Incroyable*', around 1795. One of the more extreme reactions to the end of the Terror.

C Women's fashions after the Revolution copied the styles of ancient Greeks.

Activities...

1 How did fashion reflect the political changes during the Revolution and afterwards?

2 In what other ways did life change in Paris after July 1794?

3 What reasons can you suggest to explain why some of these changes took place? (Look back at the last unit for clues.)

2.9 When was the Revolution?

Chain of Events

Assembly of Notables:
spring 1787

Floods, poor harvest, riots:
autumn–winter 1788–89

Meeting of Estates:
May 1789

Tennis Court Oath:
June 1789

Storming of the Bastille:
July 1789

Peasant uprisings:
July–August 1789

End of nobles' rights:
August 1789

March to Versailles:
October 1789

End of nobles' titles:
1790

Royal family escapes.
Captured at Varennes:
June 1791

War with Austria:
April 1792

Crowd attack King at Tuileries:
August 1792

September Massacres:
September 1792

Edict of Fraternity:
November 1792

King on trial:
December 1792

Execution of King:
January 1793

Jacobins seize power:
April 1793

The events that you are studying in this book are part of what historians call the **French Revolution**. We need to ask two simple questions about this: '**What** is a revolution?' and '**When** did the French Revolution happen?'

Historians use the word 'revolution' to describe a dramatic change in people's lives, or in the way that a country is run. It often means that a great change has taken place in who runs a country. This is called a change in **political power** when the power to run a country shifts from one group of people to another. It often happens over a fairly short period of time and so the change is quite sudden.

There was a revolution in Britain in the 1640s when Parliament overthrew King Charles I. There was another in 1688 when Parliament overthrew King James II. People even call the changes which happened in Britain in the 18th century the **Industrial** and **Agricultural Revolutions** because they caused great changes to people's lives even though the government was not overthrown. The French Revolution was a dramatic change in who ran France, which affected the lives of many people.

It is harder to decide **when** it happened. This is because it is difficult to pick on one particular event and say that from that point in time there was no going back; from that moment onwards a dramatic change had to take place. The timeline shows some of the vital events of the French Revolution.

A financial crisis started the chain of events that led up to the upheaval of 1789. For several years the royal government had covered its debts with loans.

From 'Voices of the French Revolution', edited by R. Cobb and C. Jones, 1988.

French involvement in the American War of Independence (1776–83) was enormously expensive and helped to bring about the bankruptcy of the French government.

From 'Past into Present' by M. Carter, C. Culpin and N. Kinloch, 1989.

The break with the past came when the Convention voted for the execution of the King in January 1793.

From 'History of the World' by J. Roberts, 1980.

Activities...

1 a Look at the Chain of Events. Pick the date at which **you** think that the Revolution started. Explain your choice.

  b Pick the date during the Revolution when you think that there was 'no going back'. Explain how you made your choice.

2 Look at the sources. Could you use these as a way of finding out when the Revolution really happened? Explain your answer.

3 a Choose any five events from the Chain of Events. Explain how they worked together to cause the Revolution.

  b Choose two of the following: the King, peasants, nobles, middle class. Using the Chain of Events say whether things got better or worse for them between 1787 and 1793.

2.10 Why was there a Revolution?

Historians are very interested in **why** something happens. There are often a number of these **causes**. Some are **long-term causes**. Others are **short-term causes**. Some causes are about the way power is used (**political causes**). Some are about the lifestyles and standards of living experienced by people (**social causes**). Some are about the way that wealth is shared and who does the work (**economic causes**).

Historians do not always agree which causes are the most important. Different historians may have different **interpretations** of the importance of past events.

In this unit are reminders of some of the things which helped lead to the French Revolution. Each is a different kind of **cause**. Some happened during 1789. Others had been going on for some time before that year. Not all the possible causes of the Revolution are shown here.

King Louis XIV had a very rich lifestyle.

Activities...

1 Write the following titles:
   • Economic Cause
   • Political Cause
   • Social Cause.
   Choose causes from this unit to go under each of these headings. Then explain what this cause was all about and why you have chosen it.

2 Look at the causes of the French Revolution shown in this unit. In pairs decide which one you think was the most important. Then prepare a brief talk on why you chose this one.

3 Can you think of any causes of the Revolution **not** shown in this unit? List as many as you can think of.

4 Draw a cartoon explaining how the causes in this unit worked together to start a revolution.

The King tried to stop the Third Estate from complaining about the running of France, but they swore the Tennis Court Oath to stand against the power of the King and the other Estates.

Causes of the French Revolution

The people of Paris stormed the Bastille and the protest against the way France was run became violent revolution.

The First and Second Estates lived well, while life was hard for the Third Estate.

The money problems faced by the King in 1786.

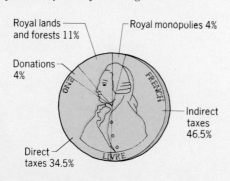

Royal lands and forests 11%

Royal monopolies 4%

Donations 4%

Indirect taxes 46.5%

Direct taxes 34.5%

Income
472 million livres

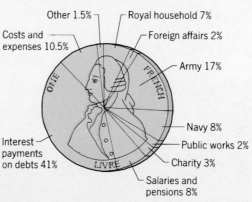

Other 1.5%

Royal household 7%

Costs and expenses 10.5%

Foreign affairs 2%

Army 17%

Navy 8%

Public works 2%

Charity 3%

Interest payments on debts 41%

Salaries and pensions 8%

Expenditure
633 million livres

Income

Spending

472 million livres

633 million livres

3.1 Napoleon's Rise to Power

Military hero

Napoleon Bonaparte was born at Ajaccio in **Corsica** on
15 August 1769, the second son of a lawyer. France had taken
over Corsica, from Italy, in the year before Napoleon's birth. In
1778 he was sent to school in France. His teachers noticed that
he was very good at science and mathematics. In 1784 he went
to the military school in Paris and a year later joined an artillery
regiment of the French army.

Napoleon was in Paris during the revolutionary summer of
1789. He won fame in 1793 at the **siege of Toulon**. The
English navy had landed troops, who had captured the town.
Napoleon was in command of the French army gunners who
bombarded the English and forced them to withdraw from
Toulon. The revolutionary government, known as the
Directory, was very grateful to Napoleon and he was rapidly
promoted.

In 1795 he again attracted attention by his energy and
decisiveness in putting down a pro-royalist revolt in Paris (the
Vendémaire). In recognition of his services to the government
he was promoted to Major General.

The Directory

After the fall of Robespierre in July 1794, a
new group took over the government of
France. They were called the **Directory**. Five
Directors, backed by two **Councils**, were
given the power to pass and enforce laws.

*'Battle of the Pyramids', a painting by
Baron Antoine Gros in 1810.*

A SOURCE

In February 1796, Napoleon was put in charge of the French army which was fighting the Austrians in Italy. He won a series of battles, and in 1797 the Austrians had to sign a ceasefire at **Leoben**. Napoleon was put in charge of organizing the peace treaty at **Campo Formio** later in that same year. He returned to Paris a hero because his victories seemed to have brought peace.

The Egyptian campaign

Instead of awaiting further events in France, Napoleon persuaded the Directory to agree to an expedition to **Egypt**. The aim was to threaten English power and trade in the area. Napoleon also hoped for an easy victory over the weak army of the Egyptians.

Napoleon set sail from Toulon in May 1798 and defeated the Egyptians in a hard fought battle. He gave it the romantic title of the **Battle of the Pyramids**. Reports of Napoleon's triumph in Egypt found their way back to France. Storybooks told heroic tales of Napoleon's brave deeds. Paintings like Source A were commissioned. There was a craze for 'Egyptian' fashions.

The actual situation in Egypt was less glamorous. Napoleon's early success had evaporated. His army was ravaged by sickness and plague. The English navy, led by **Nelson**, defeated the French navy at the **Battle of Aboukir Bay** in August 1798. The whole expedition was in danger of collapse.

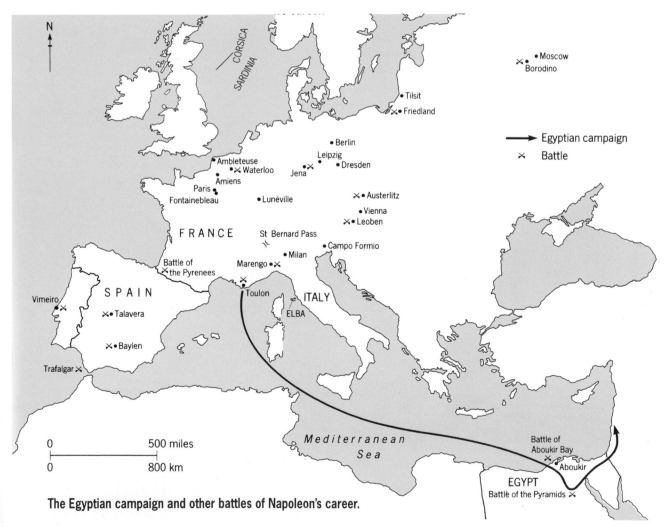

The Egyptian campaign and other battles of Napoleon's career.

Return to France

Napoleon, hearing that there were problems with the Directory in France, left his troops and returned in secret to Paris in October 1799, perhaps sensing that he had a chance to win power for himself.

When Napoleon arrived back in Paris, he was invited to join a plot to overthrow the Directors and close down the Councils. The aim was to set up a new, stronger government. Napoleon agreed.

B

SOURCE

Never was there a man more fascinating when he chose to be. One phrase explains the price he was ready to pay for success. 'When I need anyone,' he said, 'I don't make too fine a point about it; I would kiss his foot.'

He had an astonishing memory for places. The numbers of his regiments, the baggage battalions. He knew where each one was, when it started, when it should arrive at its destination.

From 'Memoirs of General de Caulaincourt, Duke of Vicenza, 1812–13'. The Duke of Vicenza was one of Napoleon's closest colleagues.

The *Brumaire*

Napoleon seized power in a *coup* (takeover), called *Brumaire*. His task was made easier because:

- The Directory was unpopular. There had been inflation and shortages of food. Some of the poorer people of Paris felt that the Directors did not care about the poor.
- Many people were tired of the years of war. A strong ruler was needed to bring peace.
- Napoleon had a reputation as a military hero. Compared with the exciting exploits of the dashing young General Bonaparte, the Directory seemed rather dull.

C

SOURCE

The Corsican Crocodile dissolving the Council of Frogs!!!

Cartoon by an anonymous British artist showing Napoleon's 'Brumaire' (takeover of power). Napoleon is shown as a Nile crocodile. The Council are shown as frogs.

On 9 November Napoleon, by promising to obey the new government, tricked the Councils into making him commander of all the troops in Paris. The next day Napoleon's troops surrounded the building where the Council was meeting. When Napoleon and his soldiers entered the building some of the Deputies (members of the Council) shouted 'Outlaw the dictator' and crowded round him. Napoleon had to be rescued by his soldiers.

Fortunately for Napoleon his brother Lucien (who was president of one of the Councils) didn't lose his nerve. He ordered the soldiers to go back into the hall and restore order. They obeyed his commands. The Deputies had to run for their lives.

The Directory was overthrown and replaced by a new government. Napoleon was appointed one of the three new **Consuls** (leaders of the government). He now had the power to make laws, appoint ministers and even make war. He quickly dominated the other two Consuls. The son of a poor Corsican lawyer was now ruling France.

It was well worth seeing how he talked to the soldiers. He questioned them one after the other about the battles they had fought and their wounds. He was in the habit of reading the lists of the soldiers at night before he slept. He kept these names in a corner of his memory, and this helped him when he wanted to recognize a soldier and give him the pleasure of a cheering word from his general. He spoke to the men in a tone of good fellowship, which delighted them all, as he reminded them of the battles they had fought together.

From 'Memoirs of Madame de Remusat', a friend of Napoleon's first wife, Josephine (English translation, 1880).

I was very careful. I listened to advice from everyone, but gave advice only in the interests of my own plans. I hid myself from the people because I knew that when the moment came, curiosity to see me would bring them running after me. Everyone ran into my nets, and when I became head of state there was not a party in France that did not build some special hope on my success.

Napoleon, in conversation with Madame de Remusat in 1803, remembers his plans at the time of the Brumaire, 1799.

Activities...

1 Make a timeline of the main events in Napoleon's rise to the top.

2 Why were paintings like Source A useful to Napoleon?

3 Can we trust Source A as evidence of the Egyptian campaign? Explain your answer.

4 What point do you think the person who drew Source C was trying to make about Napoleon's takeover of power? Explain your answer.

5 Who supported Napoleon and why?

6 What was special about Napoleon? Support your answer with examples from this unit.

3.2 The Battle of Marengo

Background to the battle

The French Revolution had led to war between France and Austria. Marie Antoinette had been Austrian and there was a lot of sympathy in Austria for the French royal family and the emigré French nobles. The Revolution was a threat to the old way of life in Austria because the French always imposed the Code Napoleon (see page 50) on the countries they conquered. The Austrian nobles were concerned that they would lose their privileged lifestyle.

Napoleon was popular with some sections of the French people in 1799, but others were suspicious of him. He felt that the country needed 'peace with honour' – to beat the **Austrian** army and make peace on its own terms. This meant keeping the lands the French had conquered or controlled in **Italy**, **Switzerland** and **Holland**. The Austrians did not want the French to keep control of these lands because Switzerland bordered Austria and parts of Italy and Austria had been in the Austrian Empire.

The Marengo campaign.

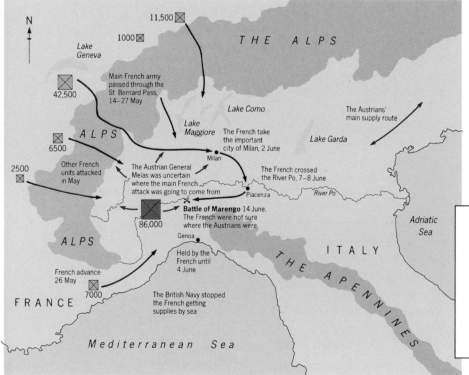

A Napoleon's plan, revealed only at the last moment, was spectacular; the reserve army would cross the Great St Bernard Pass, join the units from Germany, pounce upon Melas [the Austrian commander] before he knew they were there.

This bold strategy required Napoleon's personal leadership. He left Paris on 5 May for Switzerland. The crossing of the Great St Bernard Pass began on 15 May and was completed five days later.

The road over the pass was not completed until 1905; to cross the pass in 1800, with an army of 40,000, including field artillery and baggage was an achievement comparable to Hannibal's crossing of the Alps.

Most of the credit should go to the soldiers, the mules and General Berthier, who organized the expedition. Napoleon crossed the St Bernard on a mule.

From 'The Age of Napoleon' by J. C. Herold, 1983.

⊠	French army unit
→	French advance
◼	Austrian army unit
×	Battle

0   50 miles
0   100 km

Napoleon crosses the Alps by the Great St Bernard Pass in 1800, a painting by Jacques Louis David, Napoleon's 'official' painter. Napoleon is showing his men the way over the pass.

SOURCE

In 1800 Napoleon decided to attack the Austrian army in Northern Italy. He fought them at the **Battle of Marengo**. Victory at Marengo was one of the major battles that helped bring 'peace with honour'.

Why did the French win the battle?

Napoleon's **strategy** – his overall plan for the campaign – was to surprise and defeat the Austrian commander Melas, who was besieging the French General Massena at the Italian port of Genoa. One French army, led by Moreau, would divert the Austrians near the river Rhine, while Napoleon and his army of 40,000 men made their surprise attack from the rear.

Activities...

1 What was Napoleon's strategy for the Marengo campaign?

2 Compare the impression of the crossing of the St Bernard Pass given in Sources A and B.
  a What differences do you notice?
  b Why are they so different?

Napoleon split up his forces and sent many of them, including Desaix, one of his best generals, miles away to try to cut off the Austrians' means of escape. The result was that on the day of the battle near the village of Marengo Napoleon probably had less than 22,000 men on the battlefield, facing an Austrian army of about 30,000. Fortunately Desaix was still within earshot of the battle because he had not found the Austrian army and was not sure what to do. Hearing the sounds of battle from afar, he led his 5000 troops back in time to save the day, though he was killed in the process.

After the battle a bulletin was issued. It admitted that the battle 'appeared to be lost' during the afternoon before victory was gained in the evening. Years later Napoleon's military historians reviewed the evidence. They produced a new version of the battle which showed Napoleon as the real hero of the day.

Peace

The French defeated the Austrians again later that year and in 1801 the Austrians made peace with France at **Lunéville**. The Austrians accepted French control of Holland, Switzerland and parts of Italy. The **Tsar of Russia** withdrew his army from western Europe. In March 1802 Napoleon made peace with **Britain** at **Amiens**.

Napoleon was in a much stronger position at home in France, because the peace had made him even more popular. He was able to push through a **plebiscite** (referendum) which declared him Consul for life.

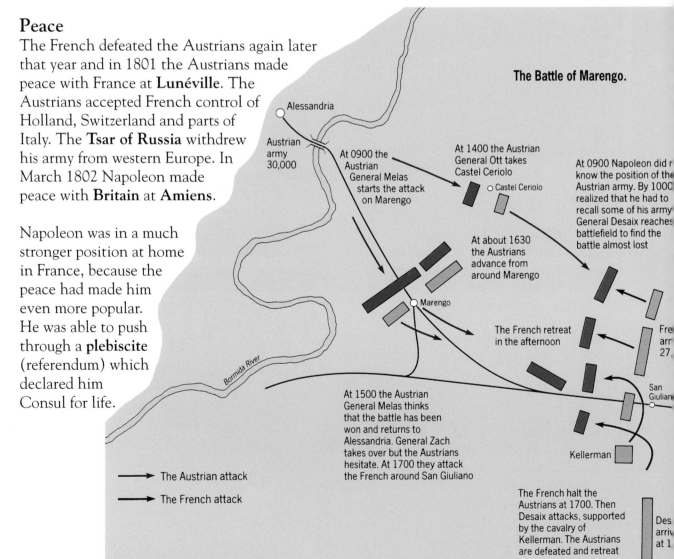

The Battle of Marengo.

Alessandria

Austrian army 30,000

At 0900 the Austrian General Melas starts the attack on Marengo

At 1400 the Austrian General Ott takes Castel Ceriolo

Castel Ceriolo

At 0900 Napoleon did r know the position of the Austrian army. By 1000 realized that he had to recall some of his army General Desaix reaches battlefield to find the battle almost lost

At about 1630 the Austrians advance from around Marengo

Marengo

The French retreat in the afternoon

Fre arr 27,

Bormida River

At 1500 the Austrian General Melas thinks that the battle has been won and returns to Alessandria. General Zach takes over but the Austrians hesitate. At 1700 they attack the French around San Giuliano

San Giulian

Kellerman

→ The Austrian attack

→ The French attack

The French halt the Austrians at 1700. Then Desaix attacks, supported by the cavalry of Kellerman. The Austrians are defeated and retreat

Des arri at 1

C

SOURCE

'Battle of Marengo', painted by Lejeune (1775–1848). Napoleon (middle) looks over his shoulder, as Desaix (top middle) falls to his death. In reality Napoleon didn't actually see Desaix's death.

D

SOURCE

Bonaparte's own share in the victory is dubious. On the day of the battle he refused to believe he was seriously threatened and did not set out for the scene of the fighting until it had been in progress for more than two hours. The victory was achieved by Desaix and Kellermann.

Desaix, after he died, received only a modest share of the praise, the latter scarcely any.

From 'Warfare in the Age of Bonaparte' by Michael Glover, 1980.

E

SOURCE

It was 5pm before Desaix arrived with his division and eight guns. Desaix attacked the Austrians. He died at the head of his men, but the Austrians fell back. Kellermann went at them with 500 horsemen. The Austrians dissolved in panic.

From 'Napoleonic Wars' by Michael Glover, 1979.

Activities...

3 How did the following help in the winning of the battle:
   a Desaix?   **b** Napoleon?   **c** luck?

4 Which do you think was the most important cause of the French victory at Marengo? Why?

5 What questions would you want to ask about the painter of Source C to help you decide if you can trust it as evidence of the battle?

6 What were the effects (results) of the Battle of Marengo?

7 'The myth of Napoleon's career was very different from the reality.' What evidence can you find in this unit to support this statement?

3.3 Invasion Britain

France and **Britain** had made peace at Amiens in March 1802 but it didn't last long. In May 1803 they were at war again.

The British government was angry that Napoleon refused to remove his troops from **Holland**. He had invaded **Switzerland** and was not prepared to live in peace. He wanted to build a great empire. Napoleon also challenged British trade and power in **Australia**, **India** and the **West Indies**.

Napoleon was angry with the British. They were still sheltering noblemen who had escaped from France. He planned an invasion of Britain. How likely was he to be successful?

In 1803 Britain had a small **army** and a large, powerful **navy** of 52 fighting ships. Napoleon, on the other hand, had a powerful and successful army of 150,000 soldiers, but only 13 out of his 42 fighting ships were ready to sail. Napoleon was a brilliant general but he was no sailor and he didn't have the same knowledge of sea warfare as, for example, **Lord Nelson**.

Napoleon travelled to the coast of northern France and chose the places where the invasion ships and soldiers would be based. He was involved in every stage of the invasion planning. He wrote instructions for sailing the ships. He even ordered a special song to be composed. There were to be 2000 invasion craft. A completely new port was built by 50,000 labourers at **Ambleteuse**.

A **SOURCE**

Napoleon's admirals understood that the problem of invading Britain could not be solved, because of the English Channel and its complicated tides, currents and fog, and because of the Royal Navy and its superb sailors and gunners. Napoleon solved the problem to his own satisfaction by ignoring the Channel and the English Navy. The army would row itself across to England in a vast fleet of invasion ships. None of the invasion craft was fit to sail the Channel in anything but the calmest conditions. The *peniche*, in which most of the army was to sail, was suitable only for a trip round the bay on a fine afternoon.

From 'Bonaparte' by C. Barnett, 1978.

B **SOURCE**

A Martello tower, one of the many built around the southern coast of England, as a defence against Napoleon's threat of invasion.

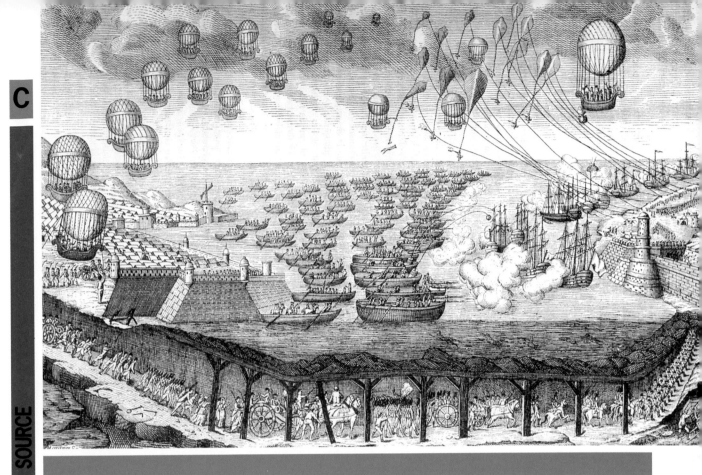

Cartoon from 1803, showing the French army crossing the Channel. England is on the right of the picture.

These preparations were very expensive. By 1804 Napoleon had run out of money, so he had to borrow money from bankers at very high interest rates. He was even prepared to make the people of France pay a new tax to raise money for the invasion.

By 2 December 1803 all was ready. Napoleon planned that his 'Army of England' would cross the Channel in January 1804. He said that eight hours of night, given good weather, would decide the fate of the universe. He waited, but the weather was not right.

Then in early 1804 Napoleon's attention was distracted by a plot against him, and by his preparations to be crowned Emperor. In December 1804 the Spanish joined the French in the war against Britain. The French and Spanish navies hoped to join together to gain control of the English Channel, and invade Britain. The weakness of the plan was shown in October 1805 when the British navy defeated a combined French and Spanish force at the **Battle of Trafalgar**. Napoleon realized that his navy was not strong enough to allow his invasion plan to succeed, so at the end of 1805 he called off the invasion.

Activities...

1 Why did Napoleon want to invade Britain?

2 Look at Source C.
   a Name three possible ways of invading Britain shown here.
   b Name two ways in which the British are trying to stop the invasion.
   c Is this source serious? Explain your answer.

3 How seriously do you think Napoleon took the plan to invade Britain? Give reasons for your answer.

4 Why do you think the invasion of Britain failed?

3.4 The New Caesar?

In 1804 Napoleon crowned himself **Emperor of France**. The poor lawyer's son from Corsica ruled a mighty empire in Europe as well as colonies in other parts of the world. Now it was time to make sure people appreciated his greatness.

During his campaigns in Italy he had seen the glory of the ancient Romans. He had also read about the lives of the Roman emperors, especially the first of the emperors, **Caesar Augustus**. This seemed an ideal person to model himself on.

A

Carved ceremonial drinking cup from Gaul (France) showing a Roman emperor driving through Rome in triumph. It was a great honour to have a 'triumphal' procession through Rome.

B

Constantine's Arch from Ancient Rome.

C

L'Arc de Triomphe du Carrousel, Paris. It was built between 1806 and 1836, and is decorated with carvings showing Napoleon's victories.

D

I mean the glory of my reign to be to change the face of the territory of my empire. Carrying out these great works is just as necessary for my people as it is for me. You must not die without leaving behind things for people in the future to remember you by.

Napoleon, in a letter to the Minister of the Interior on 14 November 1807, explaining why he ordered the building of canals, roads, aqueducts and public buildings.

E

I fought many wars all over the world by land and sea. I have been consul thirteen times and have been a senator forty years. I repaired the aqueducts and eighty-two temples. I gave three gladiator shows at which 10,000 people fought. I brought peace to Gaul, Spain, Germany and many other places. I added Egypt to the empire. The people gave me the title of Father of the Country.

From the 'Works of the Divine (God-like) Augustus' written by Emperor Augustus. It was found after Augustus died in AD14 and tells the story of some of the things he did when he was Emperor.

F

Napoleon goes up to heaven – a painting by Ingres, 1853.

Activities...

1 Compare Sources B and C. In what ways are they similar?

2 a Read Source E and list the 'great' things Augustus did.
   b Why might Napoleon have been impressed with this list?

3 Copy and complete the following chart about Napoleon's 'image'.

Questions	Source F
What is it?	
Who made it?	
When was it made?	
How is Napoleon shown?	
Why might he be shown like this?	

Look through this book and find two other pictures of Napoleon. Then complete the chart for the two pictures.

3.5 The Crowning of the New Caesar

David

Jacques Louis David (1748–1825) had travelled to Italy in 1775 and had studied the art and sculpture of the ancient Romans. Some of his paintings were about ancient Roman stories.

David was a keen supporter of the French Revolution. He painted scenes from the Revolution such as the Tennis Court Oath (page 15). In 1792 he was elected a Paris Deputy and was a supporter of Robespierre. He voted for the death of the King. After Robespierre lost power David was put in prison. He narrowly escaped being sent to the guillotine. In 1796 the new government released him. When Napoleon came to power he took an interest in the work of David. In 1797 David declared 'Bonaparte is my hero!'

B

SOURCE

David sketched Napoleon crowning himself Emperor and holding a sword against his heart. The artist explained: 'This showed admiring onlookers that he who has known how to win the crown will also know how to defend it.' Napoleon in fact did not hold a sword at the moment he placed the crown upon his head. To some observers, however, the sword dominated the coronation. One of the Emperor's advisers declared that despite the presence of the Pope, Napoleon appeared to have been made Emperor only by his sword.

Description of David in 'The Age of Napoleon' by C. Herold, 1983.

A

SOURCE

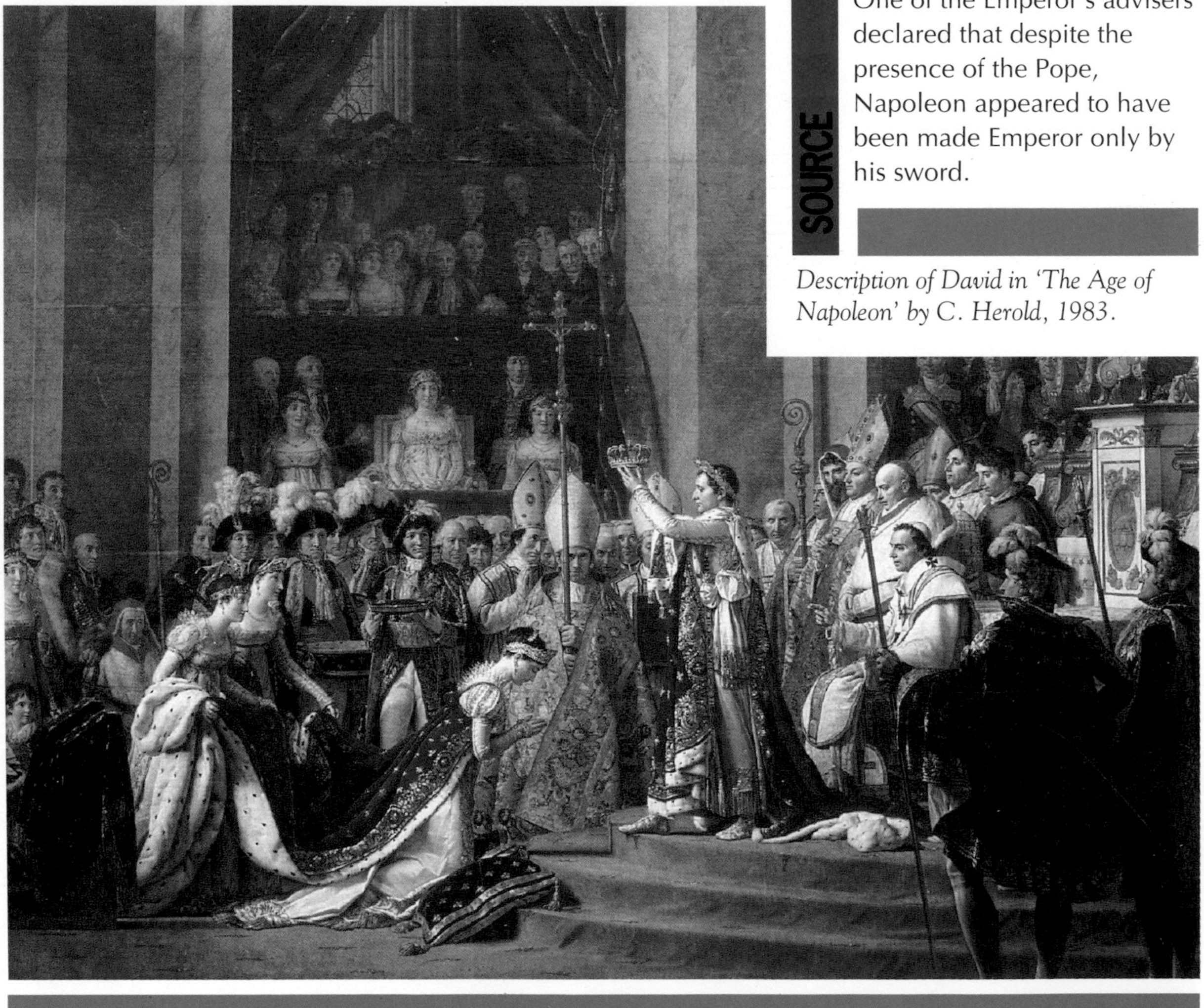

Napoleon takes the crown from the Pope (seated), turns his back and puts it on his own head. This massive painting by David in 1805–7 measures 900cm x 570cm.

C

SOURCE

Sketch by David for the painting of the coronation of Napoleon.

Napoleon realized that David's paintings could be useful to him. He commissioned the painting of the **crossing of the Alps** (page 41). In 1804 Napoleon made David his Chief Painter. David's job was to supervize the work of other artists and to paint huge pictures of the Emperor in an image which Napoleon would approve of. In 1804 Napoleon commissioned four large paintings of the coronation ceremonies.

The Coronation

Napoleon chose to be crowned Emperor in the old Cathedral of Notre Dame. He thought it had more tradition than the Church of the Invalides (the place where many revolutionary celebrations had taken place). He even ordered a copy to be made of the crown worn hundreds of years earlier by Charlemagne, Emperor of the Franks.

David thought his family would be promised a special stand for the coronation. He was so angry when he only received two tickets that he decided to paint his family into the picture anyway. They can be seen in the gallery above Napoleon's mother. Although she is seen seated in the centre of the painting, she didn't attend the coronation either. Napoleon instructed David to alter the portrait of the Pope to show him raising his hands as if to bless the coronation.

When Napoleon made himself Emperor and crowned Josephine Empress on 18 May 1804 it meant the end of the **Republic** and the return of the **monarchy**.

Activities...

1 How does the version of the coronation described in Source B differ from that portrayed in Source A?

2 Which facts about the coronation does Source C seem to ignore?

3 What do we learn from this unit about:
   a Napoleon?
   b David?

4 a Why do you think David included his family in the painting?
   b You are given a lot of evidence about David. Why are historians keen to find out as much as possible about him?

5 In what ways are Sources A and C propaganda?

3.6 The Great Reformer

Napoleon is famous for his **military victories**, but he is also remembered for the **reforms** (improvements) he made within France. How deserved is his reputation as a great reformer?

Education

- Four grades of schools were set up – primary, secondary, *lycées* (schools run on military lines) and technical schools. Primary education stayed much as it had been before 1789.
- Science and mathematics became more important subjects in secondary education than they had previously been.
- In 1814 there were still only 36 *lycées*, with 9000 pupils, out of a population of about 30 million.

The Code Napoleon, 1804

In 1789 there was no single code of national laws. There were many different local laws, which were of more help to the nobility than the peasants. The Napoleonic Code introduced a clear, common set of laws:

- people were declared equal before the law. There were no special rights or privileges for nobles, churchmen or rich people.
- feudal rights and privileges were ended.
- trial by jury was guaranteed.
- religious freedom was guaranteed.
- parents were given great powers over their children.
- wives were not allowed to sell, give away or mortgage property.
- wives could only own property with their husbands' written permission.
- fathers were allowed to imprison their children for up to one month.

The Code was introduced into parts of Europe conquered by Napoleon, such as Spain, Italy and parts of Germany. It was also introduced into other parts of the world, such as South America and Louisiana.

Napoleon had used his own skills and talents to get to the top. He tried to reward talented, hardworking people by setting up a new honour, or rank, in 1802, called the Legion of Honour.

A SOURCE

B SOURCE

Your throne can only be established on the trust of the people. The benefits of the Code Napoleon, public trial and the introduction of juries, will be the leading features of your Government. And to tell you the truth, I count more upon them than on military victories.

Letter from Napoleon to his brother Jerome who became King of Westphalia in 1807.

C
SOURCE

The view along the Rue de Rivoli, Paris, built after Napoleon was crowned Emperor.

D
SOURCE

A bride must be made to realize that on leaving the protection of her family she passes under that of her husband. The husband must possess the absolute power and right to say to his wife: 'Madam you shall not go to the theatre, you shall not receive such and such a person, for the children you bear shall be mine'. Women should stick to knitting.

Comments made by Napoleon during the preparation of the Code Napoleon.

E
SOURCE

In only one respect did Napoleon show more care for the working classes than most governments of his time: he kept a strict control over the price of food. 'I fear revolutions when they are caused by hunger,' he remarked to his minister Chaptal. 'I would be less afraid of a battle against an army of two hundred thousand.'

From 'The Age of Napoleon' by J. C. Herold, 1983.

Free speech
Napoleon did not allow free speech in France or in his empire. Newspapers were controlled and checked in case they criticized his government. He had a secret police force and from 1810 allowed people to be arrested without trial.

Buildings
Napoleon also ordered the building of new roads, bridges and canals. A lot of money was spent on improving the image of Paris. New buildings were put up and a better network of roads was planned.

Activities...

1 Who benefited from the changes? Explain your answer.

2 Who found their lives worse as a result of the changes? Explain your answer.

3 Does Napoleon deserve his reputation as a great reformer?

3.7 Master of Europe

In 1810 Napoleon controlled a huge **empire** in Europe. This had been built up by years of military victories. The map shows that only five countries in Europe remained independent of France.

Economic warfare

Britain was the most dangerous and powerful of these independent countries. Napoleon had failed to invade Britain because his navy was not strong enough (pages 44–5). Britain's army was not strong enough to invade France. Therefore the two countries fought a different kind of war – an **economic war** – against each other.

In 1803 Napoleon took over Hanover and barred British trade on the Elbe and Weser waterways, as well as in all French ports. In 1804 he stopped British and colonial goods from entering ports on the North Sea. This was the beginning of the blockade of British goods, known as the **Continental System**.

Unfortunately for Napoleon the Continental System did not produce the results which he had hoped for. The British navy had defeated the French navy at the battle of Trafalgar in 1805, and was strong enough to make countries obey its own blockade, to encourage people to trade with Britain, and break the Continental System.

Military victories

In 1805, Napoleon had beaten the armies of **Austria** and **Russia** at the battle of **Austerlitz**. The **Prussians** were defeated at the battle of **Jena** in 1806.

In 1807 French troops defeated a Russian army at the battle of **Friedland**. The Tsar (Emperor) of Russia and King Frederick William III of Prussia then met Napoleon at **Tilsit** and made peace. Prussia lost about one third of its land, and had to agree to Napoleon's plan to set up two new countries on either side of Prussia. They were the **Kingdom of Westphalia** and the **Grand Duchy of Warsaw**.

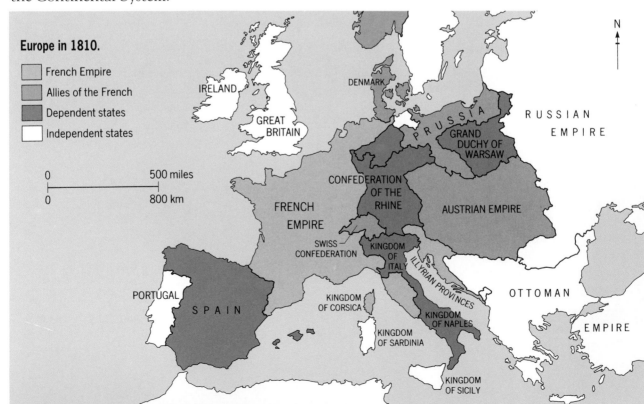

Europe in 1810.

- French Empire
- Allies of the French
- Dependent states
- Independent states

English cartoon, 1808, showing opinions about Napoleon held by people in different countries.

B Napoleon's ideas became increasingly negative. He relied mainly on the sword to keep control and felt a single defeat would end his career. He said 'At home and abroad, I reign only by the fear I inspire.'

From 'European History, 1789–1815' by C. A. Leeds, 1989.

Activities...

1 Compare the map of Europe in 1810 (page 52) with the map of Europe in 1780 (page 5). What changes had taken place?

2 What problems might be created by ruling such a large empire?

3 Why do you think the Continental System failed?

4 Consider Source A and the rest of this unit. Can Napoleon be said to be truly 'The Master of Europe' in 1810? Explain your answer.

What was the Continental System?

Napoleon's aim was to weaken Britain's economy by closing ports with which the British traded, and forcing the British to pay with gold for imported goods.

1 **The Berlin Decrees**, 21 November 1806
France, Spain, Switzerland, Italy, Holland and the Confederation of the Rhine were not allowed to trade with Britain.

2 **The Milan Decrees**, 23 November 1806
Any ship which called at a British port could be seized. Any goods from Britain's empire were to be treated as British goods.

3 Denmark, Russia, Prussia and Austria were brought into the Continental System.

How did the British respond?

The British issued the **Orders in Council**:

1 Neutral ships were not allowed to trade with French ports or with countries which had accepted the Berlin Decrees.

2 Any country which refused to trade with British ships was to be **blockaded**. This meant that British ships would stop ships from leaving port.

4.1 The Peninsular War

In 1808 French troops invaded **Spain**. Six years later they had been completely defeated and forced back into France. How did an army which had won so many battles lose this war?

The causes of the Peninsular War

In 1801 Spain and France had agreed not to fight each other. In 1808 Charles IV gave up the Spanish throne in favour of his son Ferdinand. Napoleon decided not to support Ferdinand and instead offered the Spanish crown to his own brother, Joseph, who had been King of Naples since 1806. Napoleon was determined to conquer both Spain and **Portugal**. He wanted to bring them into his empire and into the **Continental System**. **Britain** came into the war on the side of Portugal and Spain. Portugal was an old trading partner of Britain.

French problems
Baylen

Soon after French troops invaded Spain they captured Ferdinand and took him prisoner. Joseph was declared to be the new King of Spain. The Spanish fought back and within a month had forced Joseph to leave Madrid. A small French army was beaten by a Spanish force at **Baylen**. Napoleon had thought he would only need 12,000 men to control Spain. He was forced to change his mind and to bring in 300,000 troops. Napoleon could ill afford to have this number of troops occupied in Spain. They would be badly needed over the next few years as he tried to conquer more land in central and eastern Europe.

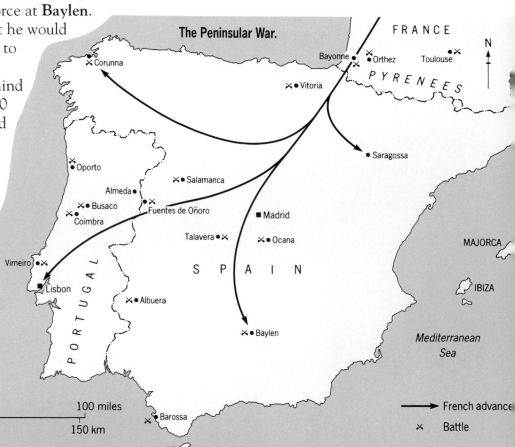

The Peninsular War.

- × Corunna
- Bayonne ● ×× ● Orthez Toulouse ● ×
- × ● Vitoria
- FRANCE
- PYRENEES
- ● Saragossa
- × ● Oporto
- × ● Salamanca
- Almeda ●
- × Busaco ● ×× Fuentes de Oñoro
- Coimbra ●
- ■ Madrid
- Talavera ● × × ● Ocana
- Vimeiro ● ××
- ■ Lisbon
- × ● Albuera
- PORTUGAL
- SPAIN
- × ● Baylen
- MAJORCA
- IBIZA
- Mediterranean Sea
- × ● Barossa

| 0 | 100 miles |
| 0 | 150 km |

→ French advance

× Battle

B

SOURCE

'Great Deeds against the Dead' an etching by Francisco Goya from a series known as 'The Disasters of War', about 1810.

Guerilla war

The Spanish resistance to the French invasion did not take the form of major battles. Napoleon's army had, after all, defeated the greatest armies in Europe. Instead Spanish peasants fought a **'guerilla' war** against the French. The peasants did not wear army uniforms and they only had simple weapons. They avoided battles wherever possible. They used their knowledge of the countryside to choose the best places to ambush French soldiers, and then seemed to vanish. Villagers who helped the French were killed. This was one reason why the French couldn't defeat the Spanish.

Wellington

Napoleon's problems were made even worse when a British army arrived in Portugal and defeated Marshal Junot at **Vimeiro**. Sir Arthur Wellesley commanded 40,000 troops in the war against the French. In July 1809 he defeated the French at the **Battle of Talavera**. After this battle he was created the **Duke of Wellington**.

In 1812 Napoleon had to release some of his best troops from Spain to go and fight in **Russia**. This weakened still further his hold on Spain. In July 1813 Wellington defeated French troops at the **Battle of the Pyrenees** and forced them back into France.

Activities...

1 What were the advantages and disadvantages for Napoleon of each of the following ways of dealing with the guerilla war in Spain?
  a Sending more French troops into Spain.
  b Executing Spanish rebels and displaying the dead bodies to the Spanish people.
  c Burning down the houses and villages of Spanish rebels.
  d Trying to force the rebels into fighting a battle.
  e Making rebel villagers pay heavier taxes.
  f Allowing villagers who collaborated with him to pay lower taxes.

2 Goya said that he painted horrible things which people do in war 'to tell men forever that they should not be barbarians'.
  a Do you think that Source B was painted for this reason?
  b Does Goya's aim make his paintings more or less useful to an historian studying the Peninsular War?
  Explain your answer.

3 What causes can you find to explain why Napoleon lost the Peninsular War?

4.2 The Invasion of Russia

The plan
Napoleon felt that he had to defeat the **Russians** if he were to be master of Europe. The army was spread out along a front line which stretched for almost 480 kilometres. To keep it well supplied, a chain of nine supply depots was set up from Konigsberg to Warsaw. Once Napoleon's troops had broken through enemy lines, they planned to 'live off the land' and take food from the peasants.

The Moscow campaign
In June 1812 Napoleon's **Grand Army** of 600,000 men crossed the River Niemen and invaded Russia. Napoleon was so confident of victory that he declared on 28 June, 'before a month has passed they will be on their knees to me'. Yet by December 1812 the attack on Russia had completely failed. Only about 20,000 soldiers struggled back out of Russia. How can we explain this terrible defeat? Whose fault was it?

Supplying the French army
Over 7800 wagons were prepared to transport **supplies**; 200,000 **oxen and horses** were needed to pull the wagons; 110,000 horses were needed for the cavalry and artillery. The supply train 'ate' one third of its supplies every day. Large stocks of winter **clothing** were not thought to be needed for such a short war.

Guerilla war
Where possible the Russians avoided fighting battles against Napoleon's Grand Army. The peasants left their land and took everything with them which might be of use to the French. They burnt other goods which couldn't be carried. This has been called the **scorched earth** policy. Napoleon had to move further and further into Russia. The Russians delayed fighting a battle until Napoleon reached **Borodino** on 7 September.

The Tsar
The Tsar of Russia was determined to fight for as long as it took to expel the French invaders from the Russian motherland. He was very angry that Napoleon had created a large country, the Grand Duchy of Warsaw, on Russia's borders. The Tsar rejected Napoleon's attempts to be an equal with him. In 1809, Napoleon's proposal of marriage to the Tsar's sister was turned down. The Continental System had damaged the Russian economy and in 1810, the Tsar had decided to leave the System.

A At one time we were ordered to buy 10,000 horses in a countryside which had neither horses nor people; then the plan was announced of passing the winter in a ravaged city where we were dying of hunger in October.

SOURCE

One of his generals describes the orders Napoleon gave when the army reached Russia. From the 'Correspondance du general Fezensac', 1812.

B Like its great leader the French army was past its best. Nineteen years of almost continuous fighting, however victorious, would sap the strength of any army. By 1811 experienced regimental officers were hard to find. Of the 148,000 members of the German army, 47,119 were boys who were, in theory, too young to be called up. The marshals and generals longed for peace in which to enjoy the riches which Napoleon had heaped upon them.

SOURCE

From 'Napoleonic Wars' by Michael Glover, 1979.

Map of the Moscow campaign.

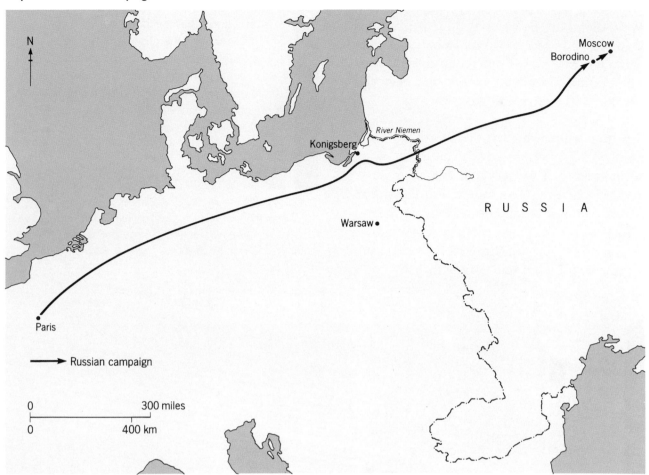

The fall of Moscow

When the two sides fought at Borodino there were terrible casualties on both sides. The Russians abandoned the great city of **Moscow**, but refused to make peace with Napoleon. The French entered Moscow on 14 September, but found almost no food supplies there. On 16 September a fire burnt down many of the wooden buildings in Moscow. Each side blamed the other for the fire. Napoleon could not use a ruined city as a winter headquarters. To make matters worse a large French army was still fighting in distant **Spain**, so Napoleon was fighting a 'war on two fronts'.

Activities...

1 Why did Napoleon want to invade Russia?

2 What were the weaknesses of Napoleon's plan?

3 It is early October 1812. Your group of military advisers has been ordered by Napoleon to produce a report on the advantages and disadvantages of the following choices:
   a Dig in and stay in Moscow throughout the winter.
   b Move out of Moscow and try to force the Russians to fight another battle.
   c Go home now before you lose everything.
In your report be careful about your choice of words because Napoleon is an emperor and gets very upset when people criticize him! Napoleon is not used to losing.

4.3 Retreat from Moscow

By 18 October 1812 Napoleon realized that he would have to retreat from Moscow and return to France. His troops suffered from sub-zero temperatures, from lack of food and from the attacks of Russian raiding groups.

How important were the bad weather conditions in explaining why the Moscow campaign failed? What did the most damage to the Grand Army? The sources in this unit provide different views on reasons for the failure of the campaign. Source A is one of Napoleon's own bulletins which gives his point of view about what had gone wrong.

A **SOURCE**

It is the winter that has been our undoing. We are the victims of the climate. The fine weather tricked me. Everything turned out badly because I stayed too long in Moscow. If I had left four days after I had occupied it, as I thought of doing when I saw it in flames, the Russians would have been lost. The Tsar would gladly have accepted my peace terms.

Napoleon explains why the Moscow campaign failed. From the 'Memoirs of General de Caulaincourt, Duke of Vicenza, 1812–13.' The general served in Napoleon's army as Master of the Horse, and travelled back from Moscow with him.

Napoleon's army in retreat from Moscow. This painting is by Johann Adam Klein, 1812.

B **SOURCE**

C Our wagons, built for metalled roads, were in no way suitable for the country we had to cross. The first sand we came to was too much for the horses. The Emperor was always keen to get things as cheaply as possible. The result was that everything had to be loaded on wagons, in the hope that we could get horses from the countryside. This had always been done on previous campaigns, but in Russia there was no hope of doing this. Horses, cattle, people had all fled and we found ourselves in the middle of a desert. Equipment was abandoned at the roadside. Supplies vanished, either because they were stolen or because there was no way of moving them forward.

From the 'Memoirs of General de Caulaincourt, Duke of Vicenza, 1812–13'.

D In fact the army lost more than 350,000 men on the way to Moscow: only some 80,000 during the retreat. It lost 35,000 men in fair weather in one week: 15,000 to 20,000 during the week of snowfall mentioned by Napoleon as the beginning of the disaster. Very many of the army's horses died of hunger and overwork before the cold struck. The sorry story of Napoleon's military incompetence was changed into the epic story of an army's courage.

A modern historian's verdict on the Moscow campaign. From 'Bonaparte' by C. Barnett, 1978.

E A storm of rain, whatever its violence and character, does not destroy the horses of an army. What destroys an army is hard work, forced marches, no corn or dry fodder at the period when green corn is on the ground, so this is eaten by the horses of the army. Winter is the time of year when a commander who cares for his army will avoid forced marches or hard work for the horses.

The Duke of Wellington gives his verdict on the Moscow campaign many years later, after he had studied French descriptions of the campaign. Wellington was a very experienced general. He had fought the French in the Peninsular War and later defeated Napoleon at the Battle of Waterloo in 1815.

Activities...

1 **a** How did the following contribute towards the failure of the Moscow campaign:
   - transport problems
   - working the horses and men too hard
   - staying too long in Moscow
   - bad weather
   - the Russians burning the crops?

   b Which do you think was the most important of these causes? Why?

2 Compare the way Sources D and E explain the failure of the Moscow campaign.
   a What differences do you notice in the two explanations?
   b Why are the two explanations so different?
   c What evidence can you find from the other sources to back up each of the explanations?
   d Which of the two explanations do you find more convincing? Why?

3 Was it inevitable that Napoleon would be defeated in the Moscow campaign? Explain your answer.

4.5 The Hundred Days

The story of Napoleon doesn't end on Elba. For one hundred dramatic days in 1815 Napoleon returned to the centre stage of European history.

On 1 March 1815 Napoleon escaped from Elba and returned to France. He was bored with life on the tiny island and longed for power again. Many French people welcomed Napoleon back. The new Bourbon king, **Louis XVIII** (the brother of Louis XVI), was not popular. The **Coalition** had broken up and Napoleon promised a return to glory. Louis fled and Napoleon returned to Paris, where he set up his empire again. His old enemies put together an army of almost one million soldiers. Napoleon quickly gathered an army, largely made up of old men and young boys, and marched into Belgium to attack the opposition. In June 1815 his troops were beaten by an army of Prussians, British, Dutch, Belgians and Germans at the **Battle of Waterloo**. This time there was no escape. Napoleon surrendered to the British.

A

I have no fear about my fame. The good I have done will be compared with the mistakes I have made. I am not worried about the result. Had I succeeded I would have died with the reputation of the greatest man who ever lived. As it is, although I failed, I shall be thought of as an extraordinary man. I have fought fifty battles, and have won almost all of them. I have framed and introduced a code of laws which will bear my name for ever. I raised myself from nothing to be the most powerful monarch in the world. Europe was at my feet. Called to the head of the government by the voice of the nation, my motto was: 'a career open to talents whatever your birth or wealth.' This system of equality is the reason I am hated so much.

Napoleon, on Saint Helena, looks back on his career. From 'The Corsican, a Diary of Napoleon's Life in His Own Words', by R. M. Johnston, 1910.

B

A French painting of Napoleon looking down on his grave from heaven.

Europe in 1815.
— German Confederation
▨ Areas of military frontiers

NORWAY
Stockholm
SWEDEN
Baltic Sea
• Moscow
Copenhagen
GREAT BRITAIN
DENMARK
RUSSIAN EMPIRE
Dublin•
AND
KINGDOM OF THE NETHERLANDS
IRELAND
Amsterdam
London•
Brussels•
KINGDOM OF PRUSSIA
Warsaw
SAXONY
0   500 miles
0   800 km
•Paris
BAVARIA
AUSTRO- HUNGARIAN
FRANCE
•Munich
Vienna
EMPIRE
•Budapest
MOLDAVIA
SWITZERLAND
KINGDOM OF SARDINIA
LOMBARDY-VENETIA
Turin
MODENA
WALLACHIA
PARMA
TUSCANY
PAPAL STATES
SERBIA
Black Sea
BULGARIA
PORTUGAL
•Madrid
CORSICA
Rome•
OTTOMAN
Constantinople
Lisbon•
SPAIN
•Naples
EMPIRE
KINGDOM OF SARDINIA
KINGDOM OF THE TWO SICILIES
MOROCCO
ALGERIA
Mediterranean   Sea
N
EGYPT

The winners met at Vienna to draw the new map of Europe. It was drawn according to the idea of **legitimacy**. This meant that 'legitimate' governments (which had held power before the Revolution) would be brought back. The Bourbon kings took over again as monarchs of France. During the next five years there were many fears and rumours that Napoleon might try to make a comeback.

Napoleon was sent into exile on **Saint Helena**, a small island far away in the South Atlantic. This time Napoleon was not allowed to make another dramatic return to Europe. He spent some of his time telling his companions about his career (Source A). In 1821 Napoleon died of stomach cancer.

Activities...

1 Compare the map of Europe in 1815 with the map of Europe in 1810 (page 52). What changes had taken place?

2 Now compare the map of Europe in 1815 with the map of Europe in 1780 (page 5). Did Europe in 1815 have the same borders as Europe in 1780? Explain your answer.

3 Do you think that Source B was painted by a supporter or an opponent of Napoleon?

4 Read Source A. How do you think Napoleon wanted people to remember him? Why do you think he wanted to be remembered like this?